Tales of the Caribbean: a Feast of Islands

By
Fritz Seyfarth

Illustrations by Dee Carstarphen
Chart Sketches by the Author

SPANISH MAIN PRESS
CARIBBEAN ADVENTURE BOOKS

ISBN 8286-0081-3
Library of Congress Card Number: 77-85646

A Limited Edition

Published by
SPANISH MAIN PRESS
Red Hook Plaza - Suite 237
St. Thomas
U.S. Virgin Islands 00802

Printed in U.S.A.

Contents

Preface

THIS MANUSCRIPT STARTED out as a series of descriptions and stories about the islands and people of the Caribbean, interspersed with personal sailing experiences—relatively short observations and tales without much organization to tie them up into a neat package. And I'm afraid that's how it has ended up—bits and pieces. I'd like to believe that it's a smorgasbord, but perhaps a more honest description is a pot-luck dinner.

The real purpose of this book is to serve as an appetizer, to lead you to further pursuits such as more detailed reading and dreaming and planning and doing—maybe to lead you ultimately to your own personal cruise of discovery to your own feast of islands, wherever they might be and by whatever means would be most practical and enjoyable.

This is most certainly not a detailed cruising or travel guide. Such books have already been written by talented and experienced people: Donald Street, the dean of Caribbean sailors, wrote the excellent *Cruising Guide to the Lesser Antilles*, Carleton Mitchell has provided the *Isles of the Caribbees*, Jack Van Ost and Julius Wilensky have compiled detailed cruising knowledge for the Virgin Islands and Windwards in their *Yachtsman's Guide* series. Rather, this book represents a personal impression of portions of the Caribbean that I have found interesting and worthwhile. I've tried to make the book both informative and entertaining by including a scattering of cruising stories and anecdotes. I've also tried to be as factual as possible, but one chapter is fictional and is identified as such after its ending.

A good friend read the rough draft and commented that he was disappointed and disturbed to find some negative inputs. I included such material because this effort is not intended as a peaches-and-cream brochure for the West Indies. One man's paradise might be another man's hell. A lot of the islands are happy, but a few are not quite so joyous; the fine people can be casual, warm, and honest, but sometimes concerned and confused. There is much beauty, but a little ugliness. Maybe there's a message for us in the stories of their successes and failures.

A great voyager long ago said that every man, before he dropped his anchor for the last time, should cross an ocean and enter a strange, faraway, enchanted harbor under a spread of sail. All the romance of a lifetime, real and imagined, comes to the fore, and the adventure becomes an emotional experience never to be forgotten.

And so it was for me.

But seven years of roaming the Caribbean weren't enough. Right now old *Tumbleweed* is being rebuilt and readied for a return to the islands to savor some old and new delicacies and delights.

> Fritz Seyfarth
> Man-O-War Cay
> Bahama Islands

New Edition Note:

Ten years have gone by since this book was initially published. *Tumbleweed* is back in the Eastern Caribbean and we can happily report that many of the islands are relatively unchanged or have modest new developments. My earlier inputs and feelings are still relevant; the area continues to be a feast of islands.

Nathaniel Butler's report from 1637 still expresses what many contemporary adventurers might find today — quiet coves and haunting harbors, many as lonely and lovely as when Columbus first found them five hundred years ago.

> F.S.
> 1988

The West Indies

There could never be lands any more favourable in fertility, in mildness and pleasantness of climate, in abundance of good and pure water. These islands have great natural beauty and riches, and in time could be made even more bountiful by many commodities. There are fine stands of cedar and hardwood, the harbours are exceptionally easy of fortification for defence against all enemies, and there is no evidence of serpent or venomous insect. The air is soft and sweet. . . . A very peaceful and hopeful place that should give all adventurers great satisfaction.

Captain Nathaniel Butler
H.M. Frigate, *Nicodemus*
Nevis, July 1637

THE TWO HUNDRED and fifty islands gently scattered in a five-hundred-mile arc from the Virgin Islands to Grenada—the Lesser Antilles of the eastern Caribbean Sea—are an unbeatable cruising area of balmy trade-wind weather, secluded coves, sparkling beaches, and warm, crystal-clear water.

The islands in this chain of jewels come in quite an assortment of sizes and shapes and personalities. Some are high, lush volcanic islands with jagged peaks almost always enshrouded by rain clouds; others are small, flat, dry, and windswept coral atolls surrounded by reefs alive with fish. And many combine the features of both. But each has its own individual character—its own brand of physical beauty and its own back-

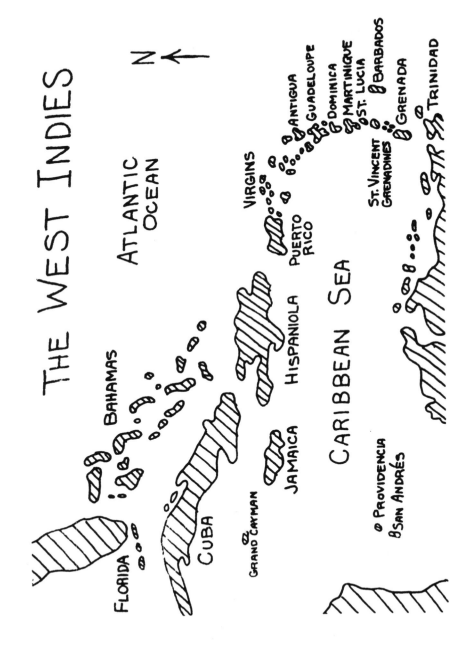

THE WEST INDIES

ATLANTIC
OCEAN

N

BAHAMAS

FLORIDA

CUBA

GRAND CAYMAN

JAMAICA

HISPANIOLA

VIRGINS

PUERTO
RICO

CARIBBEAN SEA

PROVIDENCIA

SAN ANDRÉS

ANTIGUA

GUADELOUPE

DOMINICA

MARTINIQUE

ST. LUCIA

BARBADOS

ST. VINCENT

GRENADINES

GRENADA

TRINIDAD

ground and history molded by the French, Spanish, Dutch, Danish, and English settlers who came to these islands centuries ago.

Weather conditions are almost perfect, with both winter and summer controlled by the northeast trade wind system, providing natural air conditioning twenty-four hours a day. Temperatures range from the mid-eighties during the day to the low seventies at night. Fog is unknown; humidity averages a moderate 60 to 70 percent; water temperature is around seventy-eight degrees; and there are relatively few bugs. It all adds up to very pleasant living, simple and comfortable, either on a boat or ashore.

The ever-present trades average about fifteen knots and provide glorious sailing—it's possible to cruise the islands month after month without an engine. At times the winds can pipe up quite a bit more, giving vigorous passages, and it can get wet, but the water and sun are always warm.

The potential hurricane season is July through October, but fortunately the Lesser Antilles is not as great a danger area as the Gulf Coast, Florida, or the East Coast. Should the need arise, you can find numerous good hurricane holes to snug into.

Beneath the water is a fascinating new world that is easy to explore. All you need are mask, snorkel, and fins; expensive and cumbersome scuba gear isn't necessary because excellent reef development and fish life can almost always be found in less than ten feet of water.

"Paradise" has its flaws, of course. By monetary standards, the great majority of the Caribbean people are rather poor, and it can sometimes make the visitor uneasy to live in relative luxury surrounded by tin-roofed shacks and shantytowns. What the average tourist spends in a week can represent the total annual dollar income of a native worker. But there is little of the depressing urban brand of poverty. The wants of the people are simple, and nature is kind. For the most part, the West Indians are a gentle, happy, friendly people of quiet dignity.

Poverty is a relative thing. Through the years, many of the islands have known short-lived peaks of prosperity, but seldom any plateaus. Things like steady employment, regular paychecks, savings accounts, or retirement funds are unknown to the great majority of the West Indian people. During hard times, they could fall from no great height because they had not climbed very high. In the usual sense of the word, poverty means a scarcity of money and of those things that can be acquired only with money. In modern, developed societies, this takes in just about everything. But the West Indians, for the most part thinly scattered over a large archipelago, need very little actual money to obtain the bare essentials of life. All the materials for an adequate shelter are provided by nature, almost on the spot. The soil, although sometimes reluctant to produce abundant crops on the smaller dry islands, seldom fails to provide from a small garden all that a family needs, and with only a little effort on the part of the farmer. From the sea that is always near by, a boy in a few hours can gather sufficient healthy protein to feed a household for several days. So there is no need for starvation or breadlines in the West Indies. Just as nature has seemingly set a limit above which most of the islanders have not been able to climb, so it has provided a base line below which they cannot sink.

Racially, there have been few problems except in isolated cases. Small incidents have been publicized out of proportion. A few distorted reports of violence might give the impression that the islands in the eastern Caribbean are a powder keg with a short, fast-burning fuse. Fortunately, this violence is localized, yet it represents the kinds of political, social, and economic upheavals and misunderstandings that are occurring in many places throughout the world. The few problem areas in the West Indies are heavily overbalanced by the vast majority of relatively untroubled islands, both large and small, such as Montserrat, St. Barthélemy ("St. Barts"), Martinique, Barbados, St. Vincent, and Bequia.

Increasingly, "progress" is coming to the islands. Some of it is good, but many of the recent changes are creating serious problems. Healthy and proper tourism can be an asset for all concerned; the beauty and hospitality of the islands can be marketed as valuable natural resources— but they are not to be exploited. Many of the islands are ideally suited to small hotel/cottage/inn developments; the logistics of building and operating these smaller units can usually be made compatible with the nature and life style of the island and its people. The average West Indian is certainly more comfortable working in such a low-key establishment than he is in a three-hundred-room chain hotel complex.

But the greed and/or ignorance of some opportunists can provoke situations that breed unhappiness and misunderstanding between islanders and visitors. The large hotel operations seem to sprout arrogance and thoughtlessness. The cleaning is done badly; the service is slow and poor; there are few honest smiles. The customer gets angry because, for the price he is paying, he expects the best in service and cleanliness. He becomes overbearing and insulting, and animosity and misunderstanding develop on both sides. The islander finds little pleasure in his work; the visitor finds little pleasure in his vacation.

The early history and economy of the West Indies were based on slavery; the alien businessman and visitor sometimes face a ticklish situation when dealing with a proud, free people who are sensitive to any possibility of reverting to "slave" status.

It doesn't have to be this way, and fortunately many islands are free of the unhealthy international-style multiunit developments with their premium on size and high volume customer turnover. Winds of change are blowing through the islands and they are not winds of revolution, but rather of enlightened self-interest that should prove as wholesome for visitors as for the islanders themselves. A tourism is being created that comes from within instead of being laid on from without. Small hotels and inns are being emphasized, owned and operated by local people, served by local produce, giving visitors the benefit of fresh and unique and imaginative foods. Foreign residents are being encouraged—people who will build homes and live on an island. Jet-set tourists passing through for a few days are not being enticed. The people who move to the area pick their island for its relative simplicity, tranquillity, and beauty; they are interested in the people and the land and want to be a part of it, sharing experiences. Their building and spending provide a nominal but healthy boost to the economy. This is a fine theory, perhaps idealistic, but it seems to be working on some of the islands.

Politically, the Lesser Antilles are quite a tossed salad. The U.S. Virgin Islands have territorial status and pretty much govern themselves, but they get considerable stateside advice and economic aid. The British Virgins are still part of the Commonwealth but have the distinction of using the U.S. dollar as their official currency. The rest of the former

British islands (such as Antigua, St. Lucia, Barbados, St. Vincent, Grenada) are now independent states and govern themselves completely, although they still have some ties to England. Since they are essentially new little countries, they are a bit unstable politically and economically.

Martinique, Guadeloupe, St. Barts, and half of St. Martin are still French colonies. St. Eustatius ("Statia"), Saba and the other half of St. Martin are Dutch colonies.

During the past four hundred years, the original West Indians (the Caribs and Arawaks) have been replaced by people from every continent of the world. A turbulent history has resulted in quite a melding of cultures, nations, languages, and races. But large or small and whatever the nationality, the Isles of the Caribees still weave their magic—whether it's the action of St. Thomas and Martinique or the isolated and tranquil beauty of the Tobago Cays and World's End Reef. All provide an endless supply of nerve-soothing sea, sand, and sun.

And the cruising sailor can have the best of all worlds, roaming the islands at a leisurely pace, carrying his home with him as he explores and enjoys the nearly boundless natural delights of weather, geography, and people. Under sail, this string of islands offers rail-down channel crossings and easy, smooth-water glides down lush lee shores.

These islands are a tropical world of flowering highlands and sparkling underwater reef gardens, of boiling volcanoes, hidden waterfalls, and spring-fed lagoons. They offer quiet coves and haunting harbors, many still as lonely and lovely as when Columbus first found them centuries ago.

The Virgin Islands

NO AREA ANYWHERE in the world offers better cruising than the Virgins, with some hundred islands and cays sprinkled over an area forty miles long and ten miles wide in the northeast corner of the Caribbean Sea. The western third of this delightful patchwork belongs to the United States; the remainder is British. The Virgins are rugged, mountainous islands rising sharply from the sea, but they are not particularly lush. The climate is relatively dry and the land is short of towering forests and cascading streams. Much of the beauty is in the islands' outlines: peaks, ridges, and cliffs against clear blue skies and white trade-wind clouds, and shorelines of small bays, hidden coves, bright beaches, and warm, clean water.

When Columbus first saw the islands on his second voyage to the New World, he named them Las Virgenes after the eleven thousand virgins of St. Ursula. Seven flags have provided the islands with a varied background—Spanish, British, Dutch, French, Knights of Malta, Danish, U.S.—and traces of each culture are still visible.

In the commercial harbors of St. Thomas, St. Croix, and Tortola, schooners and interisland freight boats unload at the waterfront. Open trucks and carts piled high with wares rumble off to dim shops. A native sloop under sail tacks into the habor, its deck overflowing with bananas, oranges, and sacks of potatoes, and a goat tied to the mainmast.

Here remains one of the last strongholds of commercial sail. The strong, sweet smell of rum in casks mingles with the rich aromas of coffee and spices and fresh fruits as cargoes arrive from all over the West Indies. Sailors sing to a calypso beat as they sew patches to heavy canvas sails and vocally ogle the short-skirted girls strolling along the crowded quay.

Through the centuries St. Thomas has been the destination of a

The Virgin Islands

VIRGIN GORDA

N ←

GUANA

CAMANOE

BEEF

TORTOLA

PETER

NORMAN

JOST VAN DYKE

BRITISH
U.S.

ST. JOHN

ST. THOMAS

↓ To St. Croix

variety of seafarers, due in part to the delights of her shore. As early as 1765 Charlotte Amalie was declared a free port by the king of Denmark and soon became not only a center of legitimate trade for the West Indies but a rendezvous of soldiers-of-fortune and buccaneers, including that infamous and colorful rascal Edward Teach, better known as Blackbeard. He was a massive man noted for his boldness, fiendish appearance, and roguish ways. Sporting a pair of cutlasses, three brace of pistols, and a musket, he was a walking arsenal with an appearance designed to make any adversary immediately beg for mercy. Thickly matted with blood and food, his long black beard was sometimes braided with brightly colored ribbons and turned about his ears. Slow burning cords tucked under his hat wreathed his head with demonic smoke. All this, together with his fierce and wild eyes, "made him such a figure that imagination cannot form an idea of a fury from hell to look more frightful." Blackbeard's favorite pastime was to create a version of hell by battening down the hatches of his vessel, igniting several pots filled with sulfur, and seeing who among his crew could take it the longest. Blackbeard always won and was quite pleased that he was better fitted than anyone else to live in hell.

Teach was a cunning devil, and one of his filibustering tactics was to show false colors and move in on his prey in complete surprise. He usually went to great lengths to disguise the identity of his vessel, sometimes even to the point of having the crew wear women's clothing and prance around deck with parasols. Then at the very moment of actual attack, this cutthroat would suddenly raise a large blood-red streamer pennant, his personal flag that signified courage, violence, and death. Leaping onto the deck of a doomed ship, he slashed wildly with a ten-pound cutlass until the crew cried for mercy or lay dead. On several occasions, when no proper enemy ship had been encountered for several weeks, Teach attacked and plundered another pirate vessel just to stay in shape and make something of the voyage. Such an act was considered morally illegal in the buccaneer code of ethics; it was raw piracy at its worst. But for Blackbeard, it was just some more challenging fun and games. Ultimately, his head decorated the bowsprit of a Royal Navy frigate in Carolina waters.

At sea, these swashbuckling freebooters were capable of frightful deeds, defying all the forces of law and order, even death itself. But St. Thomas provided an explosive release of tension after the discipline and hazards of the high seas, and they turned to the basic pleasures of liquor and flesh. The treasures for which they had risked their lives were squandered and debauched in Charlotte Amalie's rum shops and brothels; there was continuous drinking and dancing and singing and fighting and love-making. Most of them set out on a new voyage as poor as they had begun the voyage before.

Today, Charlotte Amalie entertains a new breed of swashbucklers, and she lives for and on the ever-increasing throng of tourists—late, carefree, sparkling nights; blurry, hungover mornings. At seven-thirty a cruise ship quietly slips into the harbor. A single car moves slowly along the strand. The only real noises so far are crowing roosters, barking dogs, a fisherman's outboard motor, children's laughter. At seven-forty a jet roars overhead, skimming the hilltops, apparently a signal for the waterfront bars to unshutter their doors and provide sedation for shaking hands and aching heads. At seven-forty-five another huge three-thousand-passenger floating city anchors in the outer harbor. Swarms of cars and taxis suddenly appear out of the crevices; a raucous roaring and honking and screeching echoes off the hillsides. Four more cruise ships arrive. It will be a big day for St. Thomas. The narrow streets will soon be jammed with thousands of bargain-hunting visitors elbowing their way into the little free-port shops: pink faces, funny hats, bulging shorts—and fat wallets. So Charlotte Amalie grimaces, throws down a double shot of rum, then prepares herself for another onslaught. And she looked so pretty last night.

South of St. Thomas, St. Croix has added two large industrial complexes on her south shores: a Harvey Aluminum processing plant and a Hess Oil refinery. Population has doubled within ten years. This rapid expansion on St. Thomas and St. Croix has resulted in the usual problems of water and power supply, sewerage, housing, labor, supplies, inflation, and crime. Paradise is turning sour for many.

But not for the sailor. Just an hour's sail from the noisy, crowded, polluted harbor of Charlotte Amalie, a cruising boat can still find the first of many secluded little anchorages from the eastern end of St. Thomas to St. John and into the British Virgins—the finest cruising of

16

all. One could spend months exploring these delights with each night in a different bay or cove. Two parallel lines of islands extend almost east and west, forming Sir Francis Drake Channel. In the words of the *New Sailing Directions for 1818*, "Nature has so arranged these islands as to form a grand basin where ships may find safety, almost land-locked, sheltered from heavy open seas, . . . the finest that can be imagined."

Distances between the islands are short and there are very few hidden underwater dangers—if you can't see it, you aren't likely to hit it.

Virgin Gorda (the "fat virgin") is one of these many fine islands, full of history and mystery and beauty. Along its southwest shore are beaches that dazzle the eyeballs. And in their midst is a jumble of huge granite boulders of every shape imaginable, rising from the sea like a ruined city. Among them are caves and grottoes, called "The Baths," in which one can swim in crystalline waters or crawl through tunnels to find hidden away an inner sea-water pool illuminated with shimmering sunlight from overhead cracks and crevices.

Perhaps a prime example of past and future "paradise" is Deadman Bay on Peter Island: pale green and blue water along a half-mile crescent beach of soft white sand backed by towering coconut palms. Just offshore is a rugged little cay named Dead Chest where the pirate Blackbeard marooned a mutinous crew, inspiring Robert Louis Stevenson's famous chant in *Treasure Island*:

> *Fifteen men on a dead man's chest—*
> *Yo-ho-ho, and a bottle of rum!*

To be anchored in Deadman Bay on a full-moon night is much too rich an experience for most ordinary mortals.

But this end of Peter Island was sold a few years ago for two million dollars. Not long ago, bulldozers and dynamite blasts started tearing away the side of the hill above this beautiful little virgin bay—the start of a 150-room luxury hotel and marina complex.

The old buccaneers are gone, but a new generation of pirates is doing its best to cut these island gems. Instead of sporting fiery beards and wielding cutlasses, these modern freebooters carry briefcases and wave credit cards. But "progress" seems to move very slowly in the West Indies, and it will be some time before these plunderers can fill all the beaches and coves and hillsides with cement and chrome and plastic.

An old story is worth repeating: A businessman in St. Thomas advertised for a new employee. The salary was good, the working conditions excellent, and best of all, the job required working only one day a week—Wednesday. A likely prospect seemed interested, but had a question, "Will I have to work *every* Wednesday?"

No Problems Joe

MY GOOD FRIEND Joe is probably the coolest charter boat skipper in the Virgin Islands. He operates off the dock at Yacht Haven in St. Thomas with his old gaff schooner *Raggedy Ann* and specializes in day-sail trips to Christmas Cove. The boat is kind of rough-looking, and everything is not always in top working order, but she has real character —and so does Joe.

One February day the old reinforced winter trade winds were really hooting and howling, and most of the captains were cancelling charters, doubling up their dock lines, and heading for Freddie's Bar to relax for the day. But Joe was laughing and giggling a she pounced on me early that morning: "I'm gonna take you on a *real* sail today, ole buddy!" He had a full charter group of six and his regular mate hadn't shown up, so I was drafted into service to pull lines and help him sail the old schooner.

"Hey, it's gonna be rough out there today," I said. "Aren't you worried about tearing up the boat or maybe scaring these landlubbers?"

"No problem," grinned Joe. "We'll give them an 'Adventure under a Spread of Sail' down here in paradise that they'll remember for a long time!"

Well, I don't know about the guests, but it sure was an adventure that I'll never forget. Right off the bat, I started goofing things up. As we were backing out of the slip, I let a stern line get away from me and it went under the hull, immediately wrapping up in the prop.

Joe went over the side in a flash, cleared the prop like a magician, and was back on board at the helm before anyone knew what had happened. "No problem,' laughed Joe. "But maybe you ought to fend us off that big gin palace."

I was too late. Our long bowsprit poked right through the big back

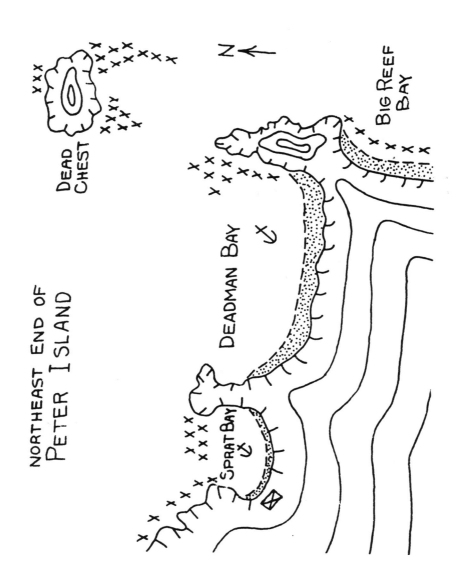

NORTHEAST END OF
PETER ISLAND

DEAD CHEST

N

BIG REEF BAY

DEADMAN BAY

SPRAT BAY

porch of a fancy gold-plater power yacht, shattering glass, tearing curtains and splintering teak, but it finally broke free. People started running around like cockroaches, yelling obscenities, shaking fists.

"No problem," said Joe. "That's what insurance policies are for. We'll square things up with them later. Maybe they'll quiet down a bit if you'll cut loose that big piece of silk drapery hanging off the end of our bowsprit and give it back to them as a peace offering."

Well, the whole day went just like that—one fiasco after another. A broken jib halyard, the main badly ripped, the foresail gaff splintered to pieces, seat cushions washed overboard. But Joe took it all in stride. And the wind blew and the sea flew. Once in the afternoon, all six guests were seasick at the same time. Joe kept them entertained by reciting little sea ditties about weak stomachs, heaving decks, and leeward rails.

> *Golden doubloons and pieces of eight.*
> *Throwing up to weather all that you ate!*

And

> *Incredible beauty, indescribable class.*
> *Look out for the vomit or you'll slide real fast!*

And

> *Weed in the rigging and foam in the scuppers.*
> *Oh, dear Lord, I just barfed my uppers!*

But finally we were back in the harbor and coming into Yacht Haven. I noticed that the "gin palace" we'd clobbered that morning had moved to the other side of *Raggedy Ann*'s dock, tied up stern-to and it looked as if most of the broken windows and part of the damaged woodwork had already been repaired. I got ready to drop sails as Joe started the little auxiliary engine. But the engine wouldn't start.

"No problem," laughed Joe. "We'll bring her in under sail."

We had a tight little spot to get into on a dead stick landing, and the wind was still blowing blue darter. But Joe could really handle that old schooner. Miraculously, I got the sails down pretty smoothly at just about the right time, and everything went fine except that we entered the slip still going at a fast clip.

"No problem," said Joe. "Just be sure to pick up the stern line off the piling as we go by and secure it on that big deck cleat. That'll spring us to a nice easy stop."

I missed the line.

Fortunately for *Raggedy Ann*, the old dock in front of the slip was rotten and broke to pieces as we crashed into it and finally came to a crunching halt. But not before ramming the bowsprit through the new back porch windows and cabinside of the gin palace. We did an even better job on it this time. The powerboat captain started acting like a wild man, screaming and shouting and crying. Then he called the police, the Coast Guard, and a couple of lawyers. But Joe kept his cool.

It was dark by the time we got things squared away and headed for Freddie's Bar for a little refreshment. A couple of the smart-boy charter skippers were still there juicing it up as we sat down and ordered a couple of double hookers of good old Mount Gay rum. They'd both seen *Raggedy Ann*'s departure and arrival, and one of them grinned broadly and asked, "Well, Cap'n Salty, how'd it go today?"

"No problems," laughed Joe, and he slapped me lustily on the back. "Absolutely no problems!"

The Grenadines

DOWN IN THE lower end of the eastern Caribbean are sixty or so little islands and cays strung along the seventy miles between the two large, lush islands of St. Vincent and Grenada. The Grenadines are the peaks of an old volcanic range thrust up from the sea. Many are hilly with the larger ones having a central ridge dropping down to a narrow coastal plain and beaches. They have protected bays, jagged pinnacles of rock, and excellent reefs abounding in colorful marine life.

Only a few of the islands are inhabited, and those by warm, gracious people, most of whose ancestors came from Africa on the slave ships of the eighteenth century. They are blessed with a climate of perpetual springtime, ample food grown in their own small gardens, and fish from the sea. They live in peaceful isolation from the worries and conflicts of a troubled outside world.

In spite of their beauty and charm, the Grenadines remained secluded and unnoticed for many years. The reason was their inaccessibility for the average traveler, who required reasonably fast transportation and a certain amount of comfort and convenience. Interisland trading schooners usually had extra deck space for local passengers and occasional tourists, but this method of travel was slow, unreliable, and uncomfortable. And there were few accommodations to serve the visitor when he arrived at his destination. The rugged terrain of most of the islands discouraged the construction of airstrips.

But recent developments are bringing this "undiscovered" and isolated status to an end. A few hours' flight time from Miami or New York can get you to St. Vincent or Grenada. Comfortable charter sailing yachts ranging in size from thirty-five to one hundred feet are now avail-

THE GRENADINES

ST. VINCENT

BEQUIA

QUATRE

BALICEUX

MUSTIQUE

CARIBBEAN SEA

CANNOUAN

MAYERO

TOBAGO CAYS

UNION

PALM

PETIT ST.VINCENT

PETIT MARTINIQUE

CARRIACOU

FRIGATE

N

KICK'EM JENNY

RONDE

ATLANTIC OCEAN

GRENADA

able for island exploring. Small airstrips have been built on Mustique, Palm, and Carriacou. And a half dozen or so small hotel and cottage colonies have been developed on Bequia, Palm, and Petit St. Vincent.

Although they are relatively modern and tourist-oriented, these little hotels still retain the unpolished, away-from-it-all feeling and flavor of the islands. Hospitality is the same as that extended through the years by a few small inns with such appealing names as Frangipani, Sunny Caribbee, and Mermaid Tavern.

The majority of the Grenadine Islands are governed by St. Vincent. A government leader, James Mitchell, has stated, "We are not anxious to grab the easiest dollar. The tourist dollar alone, unrestricted, is not worth the devastation of my people. A country where the people have lost their soul is no longer worth visiting.

"We will encourage only small numbers of visitors whose idea of a holiday is not heaven or paradise, but participation in a different experience. We shall try to avoid the fate of some of our Caribbean neighbors who have ridden the tiger of tourism only to wind up being devoured by it.

"Large super-luxury hotels with imported management, materials, and values bring false prosperity with the negative side effects of soaring land prices that kill agriculture, polluted beaches, traffic jams, high-rise construction that ravages the hillsides and scalds the eyeballs—the very problems that visitors want to forget.

"St. Vincent and the Grenadines need tourism, but we want a balanced low-scale tourism with Caribbean cuisine, architecture, and culture. Among other things, this means serving homegrown vegetables and lobster caught the same day rather than imported caviar and steak. This will boost our agriculture and keep tourist revenues from going out for imported food. And the visitors will continue to see things indigenous to the islands like cultivated fields and working fishing boats."

Possibly the most beautiful water in the Caribbean is found at the Tobago Cays about midway down the Grenadines. This cluster of four uninhabited little islets is meshed into a delicate lacework of sandspits, rocks, shallow banks, deep channels, and extensive coral reefs. It's a snorkeler's delight with forests of coral, swaying sea fans, and an endless variety of fish in a vast natural aquarium. The water itself is colorless, being completely unpolluted. The Grenadines have no rivers to carry silt and very little topsoil for the rain to wash away. The islands are mainly limestone and the beaches ground-up shells. Since there is nothing to be carried in suspension, the water remains transparent, taking its color from the depth and character of the bottom. The range of blues and greens and whites is incredible. Remote beaches are interrupted only by scuttling land crabs, darting iguanas, and plunging pelicans. The Tobago Cays are the ultimate in tropical marine scenery.

Throughout the Grenadines there's a refreshing feeling of purity: wandering aimlessly along a flower-bordered road, encountering goats and donkeys and happy children; talking and joking with the friendly islanders, who are only mildly curious to hear about the outside world; anchoring in a remote cove, natural and unspoiled, knowing that it belongs to only you for a while; gliding through an underwater world where the fish either completely ignore intruders or are more inquisitive than you are; sailing into Admirality Bay, the harbor and little village aglow with the golden light of a late afternoon sun; spending quiet evenings watching the rugged profile of Union Island against the red and orange and pink and purple of a tropic sunset; experiencing nights without real darkness because the stars are blazing in a clear sky.

Among the new adventurers who have "discovered" the Grenadines are treasure hunters searching the reefs for the estimated billion dollars in gold and silver spilled on them by wrecked galleons of the Spanish merchant fleets in the sixteenth and seventeenth centuries. But the greatest treasure of all is the opportunity to cruise these remote, sun-swept islands and villages with their many moods and faces. This is an area to be explored, savored, and left unspoiled.

Let's hope, as James Mitchell does, it can be preserved.

Passage-Making

JUST BEFORE DAYLIGHT the flashing three-second light on Frigate Rocks winks faintly off the port bow. The current has set us farther to the west than I expected, so we tack over to give Devil's Shoals a good safety margin. The wind eases off a bit, so I shake the reef out of the main and we start moving better as the lumpy seas smooth down. Slowly the black becomes gray and then blue and pink and shimmers into gold as a fine new day is born. I hear Susan rustling around in the galley and pretty soon I'm treated to the wonderful smells of perking coffee and frying bacon . . .

And now a word from Sergeant Doug Rice for an up-to-the-minute report on the county traffic situation: I'm afraid it's not a very good morning for travelers out here today. Traffic is extremely heavy with serious congestion in all areas. Motorists will experience long delays and very slow movement. A large fuel oil tank truck is overturned and burning at the Ferndale Cloverleaf. A multiple head-on collision has completely disrupted flow at the Golden Glades Interchange . . .

We should be right on course for Maverick Point, so I fall off fifteen degrees to clear Deadman's Reef. It's a real fine morning with a steady twelve- to fifteen-knot breeze out of the east-northeast and easy seas. We've got it all to ourselves except for a big schooner hull-down to the southwest. A dozen or so porpoises pick us up and play along for over an hour, criss-crossing the bow and riding our quarter wave, giving us a wild and magnificent performance of leaping and frolicking and turning somersaults. Just got whiffs from the galley—she's baking bread and I'll bet there's a pot of chowder warming up for lunch . . .

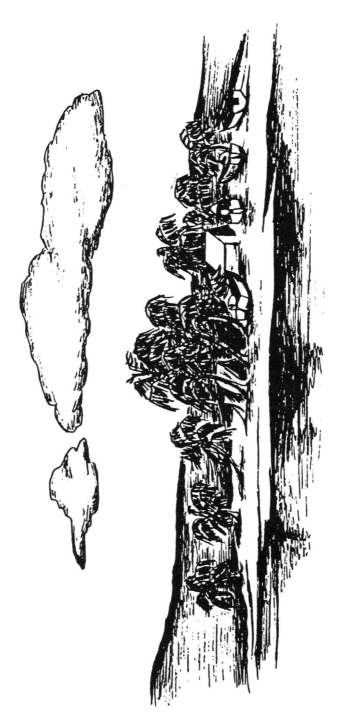

PASSAGE-MAKING

*Heavy rains and vicious thunder and lightning squalls are under-
way in the northwest sector with slick pavement, numerous accidents,
and downed high-voltage power lines—extremely precarious conditions. Nineteen malfunctioning traffic signals on South I-95 are
causing a very badly snarled situation. The Flamingo Avenue River
Bridge is stuck in the open position creating a severe bottleneck—
motorists are strongly advised to use alternate routes. A jack-knifed
tractor-trailer loaded with bananas and avocadoes has brought traffic flow on Skyline Turnpike to a standstill . . .*

It's a sparkly afternoon and we're really scooting along with cracked
sheets. The noon position indicates about twenty-five miles to go to
Conception Bay. We have one blue darter line squall early in the
afternoon and I douse the main just in time, and we drive along fine for
a while with jib and mizzen. An hour later we begin eyeballing the
opening through Dragon Reef Pass, slowly threading and weaving our
way between huge clumps of brain and stag coral . . .

*An especially heavy haze is hanging over the southeast industrial
sector, resulting in very limited visibility, noxious fumes, and extremely dangerous driving conditions. A serious 38-car pile-up has
just occurred on Rickenbacker Causeway with several vehicles in
in the bay. Wreckers, ambulances, and emergency equipment have
been dispatched. This area should be avoided. Motorists exiting Loop
10 Expressway at the Civic Center will find severe jammed conditions with traffic backed up for five miles . . .*

There's a faint aroma of orange blossoms and bougainvillea coming
on the breeze from the land mixed with the clean, fresh smell of the sea.
We close-reach up to the northeast corner of the bay into Cutlass Cove,
drop sails, anchor in about twelve feet on a good sandy bottom, then
take a long swim with some hungry, dive-bombing pelicans as com-
panions . . .

29

Bumper-to-bumper . . . stop-and-go . . . choked . . . snarled . . . jam-packed . . . disrupted . . . slippery . . . precarious . . . extreme caution . . . jack-knifed . . . head-on . . . noxious . . . burning . . .

A palm-fringed, sugar-sand beach surrounds us on three sides, backed by lush vegetation up the hillsides and peaks. The sun goes down in a blaze of glory with the whole sky changing colors every few seconds. Then the moon creeps over the ridge, and the beach glistens in phosphorescence, the trades bending and rustling the tall coconut palms, a distant roar of the reef. A tad of rum, some guitar strumming, a few songs—and then we sleep in the cockpit under a blanket of stars . . .

Bequia

SIXTY CENTS. THAT'S all it will cost you to get to Bequia. From St.
Vincent, that is, by one of several trading schooners that sail daily across
the ten-mile channel separating the two islands—*Sea Hawk, Whistler,* or
Friendship Rose.

Passengers find a place on deck among piles of lumber, sacks of
cement, crates of chickens, stalks of bananas, squealing pigs, cases of
Ju-C pop and Heineken beer. Don't worry about looking for life jackets.
They probably exist, but the captain is a careful man—he usually stores
them ashore to prevent mildew.

Bequia is an island of true sailors. Two-thirds of her men go to sea
on trading schooners, English banana freighters, or modern bulk carriers.
Most of those who remain fish or build sailing vessels from native cedar,
using only hand tools.

The main community is the village of Port Elizabeth in Admiralty
Bay. Well protected, with good holding ground and clear water, it's a
working harbor, fascinating and delightful in both its natural and human
scenery. The forested hills are lightly sprinkled with cottages. The beach
is scattered with timbers, masts, ropes, ballast stone, and anchors, between which grow pink flowers and the green shoots of small palm
trees. Boats are everywhere. Some are just skeletons being built; others
are schooners careened on their sides in the shallow water for hull repair and painting. Anchored in the harbor are various trading vessels,
cruising sailboats from all over the world, and charter yachts.

Bequia is certainly not perfect, but what a fine compromise of fantasy
and reality!

Most of the action is on the beach. In the shade of the umbrella-
like almond trees, sailmakers work palm and needle on heavy canvas
sails and manila line. The "barber" cuts away with razor blade and

31

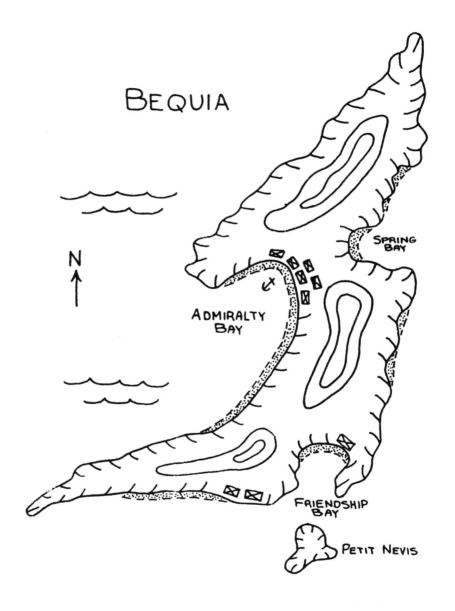

BEQUIA

N

SPRING BAY

ADMIRALTY BAY

FRIENDSHIP BAY

PETIT NEVIS

comb, the customer holding a mirror and seated on a wooden keg. The "dentist" pulls teeth with pliers—his record is fifty-five teeth in a day. The islanders don't waste time or money with fillings. His chair is an empty beer case, anesthesia is a generous double shot of locally made Sunset Rum.

Errand-bound women trudge through the shallow water and sand; neatly dressed and freshly scrubbed children chatter and scamper on their way to school. At the high-water mark, men repair old boats and build new ones. A loudly blown conch shell announces the arrival of a fisherman with a fresh catch to sell. Early every Saturday morning, a cow is brought to the village market, butchered, and sold on the spot.

The people of Bequia are conservatively coping with progress and a modest influx of visitors. Not far from the old wooden government dock is the "Public Convenience," a relatively new pink cement block building. It has three separate entrance signs: "Men," "Women," and "Tourists."

Estelle Frederick is the village baker, but you have to place an order for her fine bread at least a day in advance. She doesn't cater to the walk-in trade. Her "bakery" is a palm-thatched hut on the beach with ducks, dogs, and pigs wandering in and out. Her oven is a beat-up fifty-five-gallon oil drum fueled with scrap wood and cocoanut husks, the temperature hand-controlled by Estelle's sixty-eight years of experience.

The Crab Hole, the island's local handicraft shop, belongs to Linda Lewis, a former social worker from Chicago. She has trained Bequia girls to sew up simple beach shifts and shirts from colorful cloth and flour sack material. A water bucket at the foot of the steps quietly reminds customers to rinse off sandy feet before entering the shop.

Below the village is a one-mile stretch of relatively deserted beach now known as Princess Margaret Beach (after one of the island's well-known visitors). At the lower end of it is a cave through the rocks that leads to another tiny piece of soft white sand only twenty feet long. Overhanging cliffs on three sides give complete privacy—this one is known as Skinnydipping Beach.

A path leads from the beach up the hill to Lulley's Store. It's a rather isolated location, but Lulley has an unbelievable collection of

33

water-oriented merchandise from all over the world, including snorkeling gear, fishing tackle, knives, flags, and marine equipment. He has a beautiful view overlooking the harbor, and his kerosene freezer offers the coldest beer on the island.

Bequia remains one of the last places where men still chase and capture whales by hand, using much the same methods as their ancestors did over two hundred year ago. The Bequians continue to depend on hand-thrown harpoons and sail and oar in hunting whales, and are not likely to make any important changes; they simply prefer the traditional methods. From late January through May, one or two boats are launched daily from the beach at Friendship Bay in pursuit of humpbacks and the occasional sperm whale. The seasonal migration of humpbacks from the warm southern Caribbean waters to Arctic and Antarctic seas in late May marks the end of whaling season, and the whalemen store their gear and turn to other activities.

Whaling and boat building were learned from New England fishermen who, since the late eighteenth century, made regular cruises to the Caribbean in search of the huge mammals. The Grenadines were a favorite hunting ground for these Yankee whalemen. Each winter, large numbers of humpbacks congregrated in the shallow bays and channels of these islands to feed, mate, and calve their young. Then, as now, the habits of the humpbacks made them easy prey to the whalers. They swim slowly along the coast near shore and are easily approached when feeding or mating. The cow never abandons her calf so that she usually falls victim to the hunters if the calf is struck.

At the peak of the whaling effort in the early 1900s, Bequia supported six whaling operations, each equipped with a shore station and from three to five whaleboats. Thirty to forty humpbacks per season were taken and nearly one-half million gallons of whale oil were exported between 1890 and 1925. Whale meat was also an important product of the fisheries, with most of it sold to the local markets in the Grenadines and St. Vincent where it was called "beef" and brought about three cents a pound.

In the heyday of the industry, William Wallace, a local Bequia planter turned whaler, warned that "the day will come when there will be no more whales." He was prophetic, for by 1930 the humpback whale became very scarce in the Grenadines. But it was a world-wide situation, the result of excessive slaughter of the cows and their young by the large fleets of Nantucket whalers. Additional pressure was placed on the herds in the 1950s when Japan and the Soviet Union began large-scale factory ship whaling. As a result of this systematic exploitation, the available humpbacks dwindled alarmingly and the species is now faced with extinction.

Only one Bequia station survived, mainly through the dogged determination of a handful of aging whalemen, who kept their boats ready in case a whale was sighted. But very few whales were taken, and between 1949 and 1957, no humpbacks were caught at all.

Today, two crews of twelve men are still engaged in whaling. Their boats are twenty-six-foot double-enders with a deep V-shaped hull, and a powerful jib and mainsail. Whales are hunted to the windward of Bequia to take advantage of west-setting current and wind to get back to shore. The range of the whalers is about ten miles, taking in the nearby islands of Mustique, Battowia, and Baliceaux. Each boat is crewed by six men consisting of the harpooner at the bow, the captain at the stern, and four sailors. The harpooner strikes the whale with the "iron," a steel blade and shank attached to a wood shaft. The end of the steel shank is made fast to two fathoms of "box line" that is spliced to a long length of thick Manila rope. The whale is killed with either a bomb lance fired from a shoulder gun, or long, slender hand lances.

With the help of currents and wind, the dead whale must be towed to the shore rendering station on the small island of Petit Nevis, about one mile south of Friendship Bay. The whale is butchered in the water which helps protect the exposed meat from spoilage. Large slabs of meat and blubber are hacked away from the carcass with long-handled spades and adzes as the surrounding water turns bright red with whale blood. Several men keep a careful lookout for the inevitable sharks that soon move in on the action.

To extract the oil, chunks of blubber are heated in ancient six-foot diameter iron caldrons fired by driftwood. Pieces of fat float to the surface and are added as fuel to the fire. The melted oil is dipped out and stored in steel drums. An average adult humpback, about forty feet in length and thirty tons in weight, will yield around fifteen hundred gallons of oil. But the market today for whale oil is largely limited to local use as cooking oil and as a medicine. It is widely believed in the Grenadines that whale oil cures a large number of internal ailments.

The principal value of the humpback now is its meat, which locally is still considered quite a delicacy. A small portion of the fresh meat is cooked over open fires and eaten, but most is salted down and sun-dried. This "corned" humpback meat finds a ready market in St. Vincent at about a dollar per pound.

The sale of meat and oil from two or three whales caught annually can support a dozen families modestly, but there are years when no whales are caught. Sometimes the two whaling crews will search the sea almost daily for three months before spotting a herd of humpbacks. So the small Bequia whaling industry doesn't represent much of a threat of wholesale destruction of this endangered species.

Louis Olivierre, a rugged, bearded man in his early seventies, is one of the few remaining whalers. He knows that his whaling days are numbered, and he is prepared. "Here in Bequia," he says, "you have to be a little bit of everything to survive. I'm a whaler, a fisherman, a sailor, a turtler, a boat builder, a mason, a farmer, a rum shop owner. And at the end I can build you a beautiful coffin, then also dig a deep hole in the ground to put it in.

"Age is surely relative," philosophizes Olivierre. "I know how old I am. But I do not feel old. I still work long hours and enjoy every minute of it. Yet sometimes I figure maybe I might be on borrowed time."

One of Olivierre's friends has this comment: "I hope to hell that old coot hasn't borrowed any from me."

The fishermen frequently take a busman's holiday and organize their own sailing races. Entry fee is one dollar per man. The winner gets his money back, and the rest of the kitty goes for a rum party on the beach after the race. Under full sail in a stiff trade wind breeze, they are a sight to see—singing, hollering, sailing hard, and bailing like mad. Sails are often made out of flour sacks. The size of a boat is usually identified by the number of flour bags used to make the sail: "She's just a little four-sacker" or "She's a big seven-sacker."

The Bequia sailor/fisherman makes his living on some of the most lovely and treacherous waters of the world. He is a natural seaman in the old sense of the word. He can smell bad weather, read the clouds, and watch the birds for any changes or signs of land beyond the horizon. In this era of speed, noise, and power, the traditional and unique sailing craft of these islands are a pleasant relief. The Bequia whaleboats usually have a centerboard so they can work to windward. Rock ballast in the bilge and the weight of the crew hiked out to weather give them stability. Many a yachtsman on his sleek fiberglass ocean racer has been amazed at the fine performance of some of the larger workboats and has often been left in the wake of one of these rugged, cargo-laden sloops or schooners.

But progress is taking its toll even here in one of the last strongholds of the working sailboat. Outboards and diesel engines are replacing the hand-sewn canvas sails; hulls of plastic and steel are replacing those of pine and cedar. Although most believe that this is the end of an era, a few hopeful signs indicate that Bequia's uniqueness might be preserved a while longer. Down on the south shore at Paget Farm and Friendship Bay, sailing craft are still built and repaired in the traditional ways with the adz and jack plane. The boats have iron fastenings, deadeyes, and stropped blocks. These boats are built on the beach in the shade of palm trees only a short distance from the shipwright's home.

Without plans or blueprints, the boat builders construct their vessels by eye, using age-old rules of thumb. They decide the keel length and select and lay down a pine timber. At this early stage, the builder can visualize the shape of his boat; sometimes he will carve a small model as a rough guide. The dry, wind-swept windward hillsides produce twisted, close-grained, tough cedar trees that are ideal for the structural members of the new hull. The builder selects branches and roots that have the correct natural curves, bends, and crooks for the frames, knees, stem, and stern post. When the roughly squared timbers are collected on the building site, they are put in sea water to soak and salt-cure. This process pickles the green wood and keeps it from checking and splitting. Finally, after several months of cutting, adzing, and soaking, the actual building gets underway. When the building is completed, the boat is launched with great celebration and the assistance of the whole community.

For a year or more they have passed it several times a day and have watched it grow; they have gossiped about it, given advice, comment, and probably a helping hand, so there is a definite personal community feeling for it. The minister gives a blessing, a bottle is broken on the stem, another bottle is passed around, then all the men and boys put their shoulders to the hull. A shout is raised and everyone strains. The boat shakes, moves and starts to slide down the skids toward the sea. At the waters' edge there is a pause as a new bottle is passed around again. Another shout, heave, and final strain and the hull is pushed across the shallows on the side of her bilge, then into the harbor where she floats light and high. Some of the old people say that when such a boat is launched, the waters of the world rise ever so slightly. The months of backbreaking work are done. Now only the mast needs stepping and the standing and running rigging fitted. Then the boat is ready to be sailed to the fishing grounds to earn her price. William Johnson, Jr.

The island has four small hotels, each offering ten to twenty rooms, and each located in a very pretty and pleasant setting. Two of them, the Frangipani and Sunny Caribbee, are converted plantation houses. Spring Estate overlooks the ruins of an old sugar mill and grows most of its own fruits and vegetables. All are very casual, clean, and comfortable. And all serve delicious West Indian dishes, Bequia style: baked chicken, roast pork, spicy curries, fresh lobster, conch fritters, crisply fried plantain chips, banana bread, tangy sweet potatoes, christophine, breadfruit, pumpkin, mango chutney, coconut brown betty, guava pudding. Dinner is eaten by the flickering glow of kerosene lanterns and candles.

The Friendship Bay Hotel, down in the southeast corner of the island, allows only satisfied guests, as affirmed by the two signs at the entrance. One reads, "If you're not happy here, there are three other hotels on the island." The other says, "Our guests always bring happiness. Some by coming. Others by going."

And way down on the isolated southwest end of the island, Tom and Gladys Johnston live in a giant rock hole overlooking Admiralty Bay and the blue Caribbean beyond. Moonhole is the local name for the formation because in some lights the round opening in the hillside glows like a full moon. The Johnstons, fugitives from the advertising world of New York and Chicago, have adapted this massive natural stone arch into a multilevel cliff-house complex—a series of rock and concrete free-form chambers connected by stone walkways and porches. The guest room has only one masonry wall; two of its other sides are the solid rock of the cliff. The arch overhead is the ceiling; in front are only sea and sky. And in one corner a tree grows from the floor.

The simplicity and primitiveness are deliberate. The only ways to reach Moonhole are by boat or a long hilly hike from the end of a rocky road. "I'm very serious about making this a people reserve," says Tom Johnston. "Outsiders always ask us if we're not afraid of turning into cabbages way out here. But I made a real interesting discovery not long ago. I was listening to a group of international industrialists and financiers who had stopped by for a visit. They are the ones who have turned into cabbages."

Bequia is hard to get to; it has no airport. It also has no golf course, no casino, no air conditioning, no hot water, and little electricity. But once you get there, Bequia is even harder to leave. That sixty-cent schooner ride might be the world's best travel bargain.

Prisoners in Paradise

We all have our dreams. Without them we should
be clods. It is in our dreams that we accomplish
the impossible; the rich man dumps his load of
responsibility and lives in a log shack on a moun-
taintop, the poor man becomes rich, the stay-at-
home travels, the wanderer finds an abiding-place.

Ralph Stock

NESTLED IN THE heart of the Grenadines is a gem known as Palm
Island. Although rather small—half a mile long by a quarter of a mile
wide, just a bit over a hundred acres—it is about as well endowed as a
little tropical isle could be. The trades bend and rustle the tall coconut
palms; jade green and sapphire water tumbles gently on sugar-white coral
sand beaches, and the western strand of the island is the finest to be
found anywhere. Palm is encircled to the north, east, and south by
offshore coral reefs, and it affords a panoramic view of some twelve
neighboring islands within three to five miles. Until the mid-1960s,
Palm was uninhabited and enjoyed mainly by native fishermen, cruising
sailors, and a large herd of wild goats.

One man who greatly admired Palm was John Caldwell, the owner/
skipper of the forty-five-foot ketch *Outward Bound*, a well-known charter
boat in the islands. At the end of World War II, Caldwell took his
military discharge in the Canal Zone of Panama, where he was last
stationed. He proceeded to sail a little twenty-nine-foot sloop *Pagan*
single-handed across the South Pacific to Australia to find Mary, a girl

he had fallen in love with during the early part of the war. He wrote a book about his passage, called it *I Sailed to Australia for Mary*, and sent it to several publishers. They all returned it with about the same comment: "This is a very nice little story, but your trip was too 'successful'—not enough really exciting things happened. For a book like this, we've got to have basic gut adventure all the way."

Well, this motivated Caldwell to expand his voyage somewhat, and he "remembered" a lot more excitement: vicious storms, violent rogue seas, shipwrecks on Deadman Shoal and Devil's Reef, close shaves with cannibalistic natives. The editors now said, "John, this is getting much better. What else can you remember?" So Caldwell revised a few more times, and the book was finally published successfully with the new title *Desperate Voyage*. In one sequence he was completely out of food and starving; for survival he ate a greasy chamois skin, his wallet, and the leather tongues from his shoes and drank the dirty crankcase oil from the engine. On another occasion, while fishing, he hooked a huge killer shark with teeth "the size of fingers." When he tried to cut the monster loose, it leaped into the cockpit and almost destroyed the little vessel with its wild thrashing, nearly killing Caldwell too. His "recollections" made a great adventure story and a fine book.

Caldwell found and married his sweetheart Mary. Together they built *Outward Bound*, then set off to sail around the world. They got as far as the West Indies, liked what they found, and decided to stay a while, chartering their boat to provide some income.

Caldwell's hobby was planting small coconut palms on the treeless beaches of the Grenadines. You could always spot *Outward Bound* by its load of baby coconut palms. He was the Johnny Appleseed of the West Indies, locally known as "Coconut John" as he planted from one end of the islands to the other. But Palm Island (then called Prune, after the tough, slender grass that grows there) was quite a problem: the wild goats relished the tender young palm plants and ate them just about as fast as he planted them.

Caldwell offered to rent the island for a year from the government of St. Vincent, which owned it, get rid of the goats, plant it extensively in trees, then turn it back to the government for development. The officials had a better idea and suggested that Caldwell be the developer on a ninety-nine-year lease with the government as a fifteen percent shareholder in any profits.

John and Mary were a bit weary of chartering, and the island presented an exciting new challenge and change of pace. So they proceeded to transform a desert island into a miniature Caribbean utopia, complete with a small beach club hotel, a cottage colony, and an airstrip. And they did it with only four thousand dollars, without bulldozers or draglines or pre-mix concrete trucks. Available equipment included machete, pick, shovel, wheelbarrow, adz—and lots of sweat, muscle, and determination. Materials came from St. Vincent by trading schooner. Financing was supplied by selling property sites for the private cottages—a pay-as-you-go plan. The initial buyers were mostly people who had chartered *Outward Bound* at one time or another. Caldwell was able to hire a small group of native workers from nearby Union Island, and they became a dedicated crew, sailing to work each day in their little sloops across the three-mile channel.

And what slowly developed was no Disneyland or Miami high-rise, but rather an attractive scattering of simple, comfortable houses styled and built in a practical West Indian manner and skillfully blended into the natural beauty of the island. Buyers by that time included a British lord, a Danish prince, and a French countess.

Finally the little hotel opened. All the private cottage sites were sold; a few cottages were already completed; and six more were under construction. John and Mary were over the hump—their island paradise was no longer merely a dream.

And then their paradise was threatened. An election in St. Vincent was coming up. Caldwell knew better than to get involved in local politics, but the government then in power had certainly been friendly and fair, the opposition perhaps doubtful. So it was quite natural for him to be a bit more than just a nonpartisan bystander in conversations with his workers from Union Island. But the opposition party won, and Caldwell was not particularly popular with the new ruling group; in their eyes he was an alien entrepreneur and had backed a loser.

John was soon officially notified that his lease was null and void; he hadn't made any payments to the government for their share of the profits in the development of Palm. He presented the books to show that

42

there were no profits as yet; all income had gone back into developing costs. The government laughed and gave him thirty days to vacate the island.

The Caldwells hung on—barely. They couldn't leave their little island even temporarily, as they knew they'd never be allowed to reenter St. Vincent. They had invested many hard years in developing Palm—with blood, sweat and tears. It would be quite difficult to sail away on *Outward Bound* and just leave it.

For over two years John and Mary were prisoners in paradise. But hard heads finally softened; deep wounds eventually healed; and, helped along by another change in government, Palm Island once again became the kind of place the Caldwells had envisioned. The dream of John Caldwell—adventurer, author, boat builder, sailor, developer—has finally become a reality.

> The general impression seems to be that when white men go to a tropical island to live they automatically degenerate. This has resulted from the fact that many men of weak moral fibre, attracted by rumours of a life of indolence and ease, with all of life's necessities and pleasures at one's finger-tips, have gone to Tahiti and similar places to waste away their lives. The fact that they have gone to the devil in these places should not damn the islands. They would have gone to the devil anywhere—only it was easier here. A man of character can go to the tropics and live as active a life as anywhere else if he wishes, or he can retire to a smooth-flowing life of tropical languor that would be impossible elsewhere. In either case there is no excuse for degenerating.
>
> William Robinson

The Golden Years

LATE IN THE afternoon, she came around Treasure Point heading into the cove, sails neatly furled, a slow-speed diesel pushing her along at an easy pace, *achug-achug-achug-achug*.

She was a vintage gaff-rigged ketch of about forty feet, and appeared to be a comfortable, well-built vessel of traditional design with the proper curves and sheer and brightwork. But a closer look indicated that the hull was slightly hogged; a few rusty bleeders marred the clean white topsides; the varnished wood was a little dull . . . an aging beauty of grace, dignity, and class, but just a bit scuffed and tired.

On board were an older couple, although it was readily apparent that they were only "numerically" old. Both seemed to be in fine condition—slim, tanned, bright-eyed. But as the man went forward he was limping, and I noticed a withered right leg. And the woman wore a brace on her back. Sitting quietly on the cabin top was a fine old mutt of a dog, somewhat battle-scarred, but his tail was wagging.

They anchored nearby, he handling the ground tackle, she at the wheel. There was no shouting or screaming or confusion. Here was a team that apparently had worked together for a long time—a few finger motions and the ketch was properly snugged in for the night with no pain or strain.

Later that evening, I saw the soft glow of kerosene cabin lamps, heard harmonica music, the pop of a cork, light laughter.

Several mornings later, just a while after daybreak, I heard the rattle of chain and an engine *achug-achug-achug-achug*. They waved goodbye, and the early sun glistened on the name across the transom, *Indian Summer*.

The Attempted Rape
of Marigot Bay

MY FIRST CRUISE to St. Lucia, the second largest island of the Windward group, was primarily to explore its fabled but relatively unknown Marigot Bay. Friends who had anchored in this fjord-like little harbor usually became glassy-eyed when they later tried to describe it.

And I nearly didn't find it.

I had been told that the opening to Marigot was very narrow and difficult to pick out of the lush, high shoreline. Sailing up the west coast of St. Lucia is a real delight, and sure enough, I sailed right on by. But fortunately I looked behind just in time to see a small local fishing sloop sail into the cliffs and disappear.

So I went back, found the hidden opening, and entered what may be the prettiest sailor's paradise in the Caribbean.

Marigot is actually a double harbor. About midpoint, a palm-covered sandspit juts down from the north shore, leaving a narrow channel into an inner lagoon that is completely landlocked and sheltered by high green hills and ridges. Yet the land configuration is such that the trade winds almost always blow comfortably on a boat at anchor.

Two small hotels, the Roseau and Yacht Haven, have been operating in Marigot for a number of years. Both have just a dozen or so units. They are attractive and comfortable but apparently only marginally profitable.

In 1948 a group of speculators bought 2,500 acres surrounding the bay for a total price of $4,000. Marigot's first real publicity came in 1965 when it was the setting for the movie *Dr. Doolittle*, starring Rex Harrison. The exploiters started moving fast, and Marigot became a wheeler-dealer's utopia.

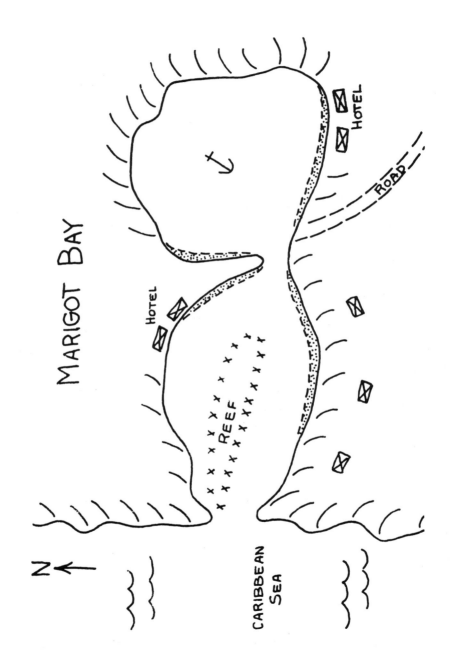

MARIGOT BAY

HOTEL

HOTEL

ROAD

REEF

CARIBBEAN SEA

N

THE ATTEMPTED RAPE OF MARIGOT BAY

One small area of less than 100 acres on the south side of the bay has been subdivided (on the drawing board) into 225 small lots at an average price of around $7,000. This adds up to a current paper value of about $1,600,000 for a tract that was worth $165 when the land was purchased originally!

The brochures and sales literature are a bit overwhelming: "In a setting of such startling and breathtaking beauty, Marigot Bay has been compared to Moorea in the Polynesian South Pacific. Towering jungle-clad peaks rise majestically out of radiant peacock seas, with sparkling mountain pools, cascading waterfalls, sun-dappled jungles of wild orchids and flowering bougainvillea. Here are the carefully laid foundations of a far-reaching community planned for tension-free tropical living."

Further: "Centuries ago, pirates, buccaneers, and brigands-of-the-sea sought shelter in this tropical paradise. Today, Marigot Bay shelters the visiting yachts of influential wealthy businessmen from the four corners of the world. But more important, Marigot can be your dream-come-true for tranquil, ecstatic living. Each estate has an awe-inspiring view of this magnificent bay and ocean. The entire project has been conceived so as to provide the discriminating buyer a harmonious and idyllic marriage with the wonderland of Nature at its tropical best."

And there are vague promises of paved roads, unlimited electrical power, water, sewerage, a golf course, nature trails, minimal taxes, low building costs, and so on.

So far, none of this has come to pass. After many years of high-level promotion, the project, I can happily report, is a relative bust. Lots have been sold (and some resold several times), but only a half-dozen homes have actually been built. One house has been under construction for five years with a crew of six on the job most of the time. Recently, the roof was finally completed. Wages are low—about eight dollars per day. But the actual labor expense is extremely high. The men aren't exactly lazy —it just seems to take forever to get anything done. And in such fantastic surroundings, one's attention tends to wander.

I asked Joe and Emily Parler, who own and operate one of the little hotels, what has kept Marigot from booming with all this promotion. "It's a strange thing," said Emily. "We've had a number of guests who planned to stay a week but left after only two days. I've worried that maybe something is wrong with the way we're operating our place. But now I'm convinced that most people just can't take all this tranquillity."

Apparently the hidden disease of paradise is boredom. Most modern sophisticates don't seem to take well to paradise, which by the usual definition is spectacularly beautiful and secluded—and awesomely quiet. Paradise—true paradise—has no radio, no television, no room service. But the fact is that many people tend to go to pieces in paradise.

One time I spent a month anchored in Marigot Bay. I guess the peace and quiet definitely got to me; I had originally planned to stay just a couple of days.

Joe and Emily seem to be very happy with the present state of Marigot. Although running the little hotel is financially marginal, their needs are simple. Joe thinks that some hidden natural power has resolved that Marigot will resist the forces of man and his complicated machinery, and that the area will remain unspoiled for a long time to come.

But he looked a little worried when he told me this.

I remember a small city in southern California where I lived some years ago. The civic leaders frantically (and successfully) worked at doing everything possible to transform what was a rather pleasant community into a typical industrial center. A roving reporter asked a dozen citizens at random if they approved of what was happening. All replied that they did. He then asked, "Do you think that it will make our city a better and more happy place to live?" And in every case the answer was no.

"Then why do you approve?" he asked.

"Well," was the usual reply, "one must always be in favor of progress."

I hope that when I get back to St. Lucia, Marigot will still be unprogressed.

But I think maybe I'd better hurry. Joe and Emily might need help.

They Sail the Islands for a Living

ONE OF THE shiniest of all golden dreams for many a boat owner—or would-be owner—is to live aboard his yacht in a tropical land supported by happy vacationers who pay handsomely to rent a small part of his idyllic life for a short time. Through the years the West Indies have been the alluring goal of many a sailor.

It's not surprising that the Caribbean has attracted quite an assortment of people—romanticists, pioneers, dropouts, adventurers, thieves—all with varying amounts of imagination, drive and versatility. But whatever their motivation, all must develop some manner of economic existence at a chosen level, be it just basic survival or a relatively sophisticated lifestyle.

The delightful fantasy persists that running a charter boat in the enticing West Indies allows a few of these lucky opportunists and escapists to stach away large bags of money while laughing and basking in the warm Caribbean sun.

"We're a dying breed," says John Sowden, who charters his gaff-rigged schooner *Anacapa* down in the Grenadines. "Nobody but another skipper knows how many ways you can fail in this business. The people who dream of chartering don't have the experience or finances to get into it. Those who have the money and know-how don't want the headaches and hard work."

To some, chartering represents a form of basic prostitution. The boat is their home, and sailing their hobby and way of life; making all this also into a business that involves sharing it intimately for twenty-four hours a day with strangers can be too much. Certainly it's not a life for everyone, but for those few who are adaptable, twelve to sixteen

49

weeks a year of charter income seem to be enough to support two people in a simple fashion, maintain the boat, and allow plenty of time to do their own thing.

During the last twenty-five years, Art Crimmins has become a legendary success in the charter trade with his sixty-two-foot ketch *Traveller III*. "Nobody is ever totally independent," says Crimmins, "but this comes real close. It's like owning your own little country. At its best, it's the most wonderful life I can imagine."

And at its worst? "It's like prospecting for gold. If it was any more difficult, nobody would do it. If it was any easier or less risky, the whole world would try."

"It's not the money," Crimmins says. "I could take what I've invested in this boat and make a much better return with a hamburger stand. Whatever we make goes back into the boat. Sometimes if we're real lucky, there's a little bit left over for us."

For most charter people, an important factor seems to be pacing—no fast turnarounds week after week, no twelve-month operation. Properly spaced, those twelve to sixteen weeks can be very agreeable. Most charter guests are interesting, pleasant people, and some long-lasting friendships have resulted. Hopefully, the guests are sharing a way of life that the owner/skipper finds desirable and satisfying. An essential requirement for operating a charter boat is that you should really enjoy entertaining people full-time and are able to adapt easily to different personalities in the close quarters of on-board living. A few "lemon" guests are bound to turn up sooner or later, but fortunately they seem to be a very small minority.

Crimmins has developed an uncanny sense about potential guests: "People who are difficult ashore are impossible at sea. I decided early in the game that the only way to work steadily and successfully was through repeat business and referrals. If somebody thought they wanted to go cruising and I could tell they wouldn't enjoy it—heavy drinkers, old people, quarrelsome couples, that sort of thing—it was better in the long run to pass up their money and wait for the right ones to come along."

He still wonders about what makes the ideal charter vacation. "Cruising patterns change over the years," says Crimmins. "Nowadays, there's less of a serve-me-a-drink-and-grill-the-steaks-just-right attitude, and more of a trend toward participation. It's amazing how many company presidents will tell you they have nobody they can relax with and let down their hair."

One measure of personal success is the number of offers for high-paying jobs that he gets from wealthy guests. "I look at most professional men who sail with me—they come aboard with their briefcases, and their Maalox, and their bulging, aching bellies—and I think, 'My God, what would it be like to be able to sail *only* one week or so a year?' The man offering the job is almost always the company president. I tell him truthfully he's got the only job that might interest me. I'm already the head of a challenging business. Why should I want to step down?"

One former competitor of Crimmins offers these comments on chartering, "You have to love the game and its bumps, but you can never forget it's a business. People go into it thinking they'll have a ball and make a lot of bucks; one season or so and they're gone. You see it happen all the time. A lot of boats have gimmicks: marine biology, scuba instruction, water skiing, swinging singles. Mine was having a pool table on board. What Art Crimmins has is a manner that appeals to rich people; he knows how to make them feel comfortable without pampering them. And to charter with Crimmins has become a status symbol. But beyond that, he's a real pro. Nothing much surprises him . . . and it's a business that can turn around and bite you hard any time you think you've got it mastered."

The two main hubs of charter activity are the Virgins in the north and the Grenadines in the south. The Virgins provide more protected sailing conditions and a wider choice of excellent anchorages, undoubtedly easier on guests and boats. And provisions, supplies, repair facilities, and air transportation are better in St. Thomas than farther south.

But with their isolation, the Grenadines offer challenging, lively, and very pleasant cruising. Most charters begin in St. Vincent to give an easy reach with the prevailing winds on down through these little islands to Grenada.

Farther north, between St. Vincent and Antigua (250 miles), the four large islands of St. Lucia, Martinique, Dominica, and Guadeloupe present a most interesting area to explore. From Antigua to the Virgins

(175 miles), there are another ten or so very attractive smaller islands, including Montserrat, Nevis, St. Kitts, St. Barts, and St. Martin.

The Caribbean charter fleet is made up of sailing people of many backgrounds and ages; the common denominator is their keen interest in boats and a strong desire for independence and freedom. The majority have broken loose from a confused, complicated, and perhaps somewhat meaningless existence in an effort to find a simpler and more satisfying way of life. They are romanticists possibly, but the more successful ones are not irresponsible, unstable escapists. Most have no intention of chartering forever. The "life" of an average charter operation is probably three to four years; some last only a season or less. Only a few have been chartering ten years or more. The ones that adapt to the West Indies usually get involved sooner or later in a small business or activity that puts their boat back in the "hobby and home" status. Even those who return to former environments or seek out new ones usually seem to have found a healthy new perspective and to have sorted out their values; the period in the West Indies has shown that life can be fulfilling and adventurous.

Mike and Jeannie Kuick operate their sixty-five-foot schooner *Queen of Sheba* in the Virgin Islands. Mike has an engineering degree from Texas A & M, and Jeannie graduated from the University of Colorado. They sold everything to make a down payment on a charter boat in St. Thomas, lost money their first few years, but managed to hang on.

Jeannie gives a good description of what chartering is like: "Take a section of your house about forty feet long by ten feet wide—that's really more room than you'll have aboard the boat. At noon Monday, four or six people you've never seen before walk in the door. For the next seven days you feed them the finest food imaginable without running to the store if you forgot something, make their beds, clean up after them, mix fancy drinks, tell funny stories, generally entertain. You play outdoors, but you have to protect them from the sun, so most of the time is spent in that little forty-by-ten-foot space. To make it really authentic, invent some crisis like the stove running out of fuel or the toilet breaking down.

"Then next Monday at noon this group, just as you're all getting to know and understand (or hate) each other, leaves. You madly rush off to the grocery store and hardware store and do all the laundry, clean your narrow strip of house, make repairs, answer a couple of dozen important business letters, and you're standing brightly smiling by the door at noon the next day, when a new group shows up to start the fun and games all over again. If you can do this for five or six months running without losing your sanity or smile or marriage, then you can make it in the charter business."

Some, like Harold and Susan Hawley, have mixed the best of two worlds. They had developed a very successful photography business together in Syracuse, New York. Restless and tired, they turned the busy studio over to their son and daughter-in-law, bought the forty-five-foot ketch *Lively Lady*, and now spend ten months a year in the Caribbean cruising and chartering. "I keep pinching myself to make sure this is all really happening," says Hawley. "Fishing, diving, sailing, exploring—and the cruising life becomes a lot more meaningful and challenging when you're looking after your guests. I'm constantly seeing everything through new eyes with them aboard. And they're paying me fifteen hundred bucks a week to play with them!"

Hawley hasn't given up his original profession; instead, he's just operating in a new area under different conditions. He has developed quite a reputation as a free-lance marine photographer, and his work is very much in demand. But the pace is slow and easy. And Susan's sketches of island scenes and people are selling well in the tourist shops from St. Thomas to Grenada.

The charter business has its losers, too. Gene and Marge Townsend were knocking them dead operating out of St. Vincent with their sixty-foot schooner *Wanderlust*. "We turned down more business than we handled," Townsend explained near the end. "For three years we averaged over thirty-five weeks of charter work a year. We were really in high cotton. But it turned out that neither we nor the boat could handle that much activity. Marge and I started fighting a lot, then were grouchy with our guests, and tried to make up for it by drinking too much. It was real easy to start nipping that cheap Barbados rum early in the day to make things look rosy. Everything hit the spin-crash-and-burn during our fourth year. We had to cancel out over half our season because of boat breakdowns and personal problems."

The word soon got around to all the charter brokers and agents that

53

Gene and Marge just couldn't cut it any more. Their bookings dropped to almost nothing. And then a final dramatic end. They were getting ready for a ten-day charter through the Grenadines. Although this was their first charter of the season, the boat was run down—very little maintenance work had been done during the off-season summer months. At mid-morning of the day of the charter, Gene brought a sobbing Marge in to the dock with three suitcases, and she headed for the airport. Thirty minutes later *Wanderlust* sailed out of the harbor . . . with the just-arrived charter guests standing amazed on the dock.

Townsend apparently was headed for Grenada, but he never made it. That night, during a violent squall, the schooner sailed up on treacherous Gran de Coi Reef east of Union Island. Both skipper and boat were lost.

It's hard to come up with a tried-and-true formula for success in the charter business. The optimum operation would need the perfect boat: high performance with minimum maintenance and cruise-ship accommodations. It would have the best location, superb food, and brilliant advertising. And combine this with the perfect crew: a master mariner, a highly capable mechanic-carpenter-electrician, a gourmet cook, a comedian with an instant repertoire of 85,000 funny stories and anecdotes, a musician who plays a twelve-string guitar and sings beautifully everything from calypso to country and western, a bartender who can mix eighty-five types of delicious daiquiris, a psychologist who never tires or shows any sign of grouchiness no matter how many times he answers the same question or cleans up another sandy mess . . . and a man who knows when to keep his mouth shut.

So naturally in the good operations the boat and crew are happy compromises. Neither quite reaches the optimum conditions. The small handful that arrive at real success seem to have an indefinable blend of affability, warmth, humor, ability, self-confidence, and composure. These few people generate an atmosphere in which guests feel comfortable, unafraid, important. And they do it without being submissive, tyrannical, or patronizing. It's a tough order—a business where the hard workers usually finish first, and where last place is crowded with the inept, the lazy, the crude, and the just plain unlucky.

Hank Patterson has his own formula for success. He is a former

San Diego stockbroker who has worked the Caribbean charter trade for over five years with his forty-two-foot yawl *Vagabond*. Ten weeks of charters a year is all he ever tries to handle. "That brings in enough money to keep me and the boat," he says. "Any more than that would start making it a grind. As far as I'm concerned, *work* is something someone else says I must do or pays me for doing; *projects* are my own doing. I try to minimize work, and maximize projects. Chartering basically boils down to being a very unique people relationship, and it's important for me to operate well below the threshold of pain.

"We don't offer any fun-and-games gimmicks to our guests—just good sailing, diving, and relaxing in what I think is the finest cruising area in the world. *Vagabond* is a comfortable yet relatively simple boat without a lot of gadgets or electronic goodies; the larger, more complicated boats are a constant drain of time and money." Betsy Miller, an ex–airline stewardess, has been his first mate for several years, and they make a team that's hard to beat. They take only one guest couple, but the charter agents say that *Vagabond* could be booked fifty-two weeks a year.

"Charter cooking can be a real chore," says Patterson. "It's very important to feed the people well, but it's pretty ridiculous to attempt to serve gourmet meals day after day out of that tiny galley. The casualty rate among charter cooks is terribly high and usually due to trying to make like a four-star restaurant. Betsy turns out easy meals that look and taste real good, but without spending all her time slaving over a hot little stove."

Most of Patterson's off-season time is spent as a treasure hunter, but so far the big find has been elusive. He mainly dives on the extensive Horseshoe Reef fifty miles east of the Virgin Islands, a highly dangerous area that has been a shipping graveyard since the sixteenth century.

Sometimes nothing works; the complicated chemistry of personalities, boat, scenery, and weather just doesn't work to meld everything together in happy harmony. Says one successful skipper, "I'm the guy who's supposed to know all the tricks; it's up to me to make every cruise pleasant. If a cruise fails, I've failed."

Chartering supported me for seven years. Not very well, but enough to keep beans and rum in my belly, paint and varnish on the boat. I was probably a borderline charter skipper; the knack of constant entertaining didn't come naturally, but it was a means to an end. Five months of real hard work and a certain amount of torture could provide seven months of my own projects. So it wasn't a bad trade-off.

Back in the mid-1960s when I first arrived in St. Thomas to start my apprenticeship, chartering was quite a bit different than it is today. These early boats were usually a husband/wife team that accepted a few paying guests from time to time as they roamed through the islands. They truly enjoyed the area and wanted to sincerely trade experiences with a few others. They owned their boats, so weren't trying to pay off expensive mortagages or amortize a business investment. Most of the boats were fine old traditional designs—schooners, ketches, cutters from the boards of Alden and Herreshoff—*White Squall, Mandoo, Barlevento, Maverick, Bounty, Aries.* These were comfortable and seakindly vessels of character that offered a true cruising vacation. The competition was very relaxed with honest camaraderie, lots of laughing and sharing. There was little profit motivation or thoughts of empire building; the only basic economic incentive was to put a few dollars in the cruising kitty for a summer of down-island exploring. And there were very few you-rent-it-and-drive-it-yourself color-coordinated plastic bareboats that today are swarming about like locusts.

Ross Norgrove on *White Squall* helped me put together a charter brochure. He wisely suggested something simple but adequate, just a brief descriptive text with not too much jazz, and a couple of black and white photographs. He also advised pricing myself about in the middle of the other boats in my size range. If I was at the bottom end, I'd probably get the price-shopping bargain-hunters who were usually quite demanding and hard to please. On the upper end, I'd get the top-of-the-line status-buyers who could also be very demanding and hard to please. Ross was right; just about all my guests were great people, Middle America.

Dyke and Inga Wilmerding on *Mandoo* showed me out-of-the-way anchorages, gave secret tips on entertaining, tasty easy-to-fix boat menus, some tricks on handling problem guests. It turned out that I needed a lot more instruction on this last item; my very first charter was also almost my very last.

They were three middle-aged good-ole-boys from Alabama off on a toot. They arrived on board well-juiced and stayed in that condition for seven days and seven nights. They had assumed that the normal everything-included charter package also provided dusky maidens on moon-lit beaches every night. There was deep disappointment when I explained that they had to bring their own salad girls. So they made up for it by swilling down more whisky. And trying to claw their way up the sides of boats anchored nearby that had females on board. They spilled food and drink, screamed blood-curdling rebel yells through quiet coves, bellowed football fight songs at 3:00 A.M., ground out cigar butts on the deck, deposited endless piles of sand everywhere, fell down, threw up, tossed glasses overboard, broke gear—but miraculously didn't hurt themselves. It was a three stooges' nightmare; I just didn't know how to handle them. At the end of that fifteen-day week, the boat was a disaster area and I was a basket case. I turned in my license, tore off my epaulettes, burnt my five thousand brochures, and swore that there was absolutely no amount of money in the world that could ever induce me to repeat such an experience.

My friends nursed me back to health, explaining that I had the unfortunate luck of getting the very rare "100-percent bummer" charter the first time out. The veterans handled such a situation quite simply: they took the group back to the dock, cancelled the charter, and refunded their money. To continue a bummer charter was a bad deal for everyone.

So I carried on, and my friends were right. There were no more bad groups. A few problem weeks, but for the most part I entertained the nicest bunch of people you could imagine, many of whom became close friends, came back several times, wrote letters regularly, sent little personal gifts. I had honeymooners (first, second, and practicing), psychiatrists, the president of the Syracuse Whittling Club, a former Burma Trail elephant driver, the French ambassador to Colombia with his nudist girl friend, an Air Force general, an ex-Foreign Legion waterboy, three window-dressers from New York City. And fine old Howard Cole, his body wracked with cancer, kept alive with a little battery-operated mechanism strapped to his chest pumping chemo-therapy drugs into his liver. Howard said that rather than dying in a wheel chair, he'd rather have it happen out sailing with me. It was a varied clientele, often quite challenging—especially the psychiatrists and the ambassador's girl friend and the three window-dressers. They were good years.

But chartering still didn't come natural to me, and toward the end I found it more and more difficult to mentally prepare myself for a new season. It just wasn't that much fun any more and I seemed to be only going through the motions. One November, after a fine summer of down-island cruising, I found myself facing the first charter with morbid dread and fear and agony, sleepless nights, violent gut aches. Twenty-four hours before the guests were due to arrive, I called my charter agent and told her to get another boat, also to cancel out the rest of my season.

Sometimes a fighter pilot is just not able to fly his mission, a brain surgeon can't make the first incision, a lion tamer won't enter the roaring cage, a combat paratrooper refuses to jump, a pirate throws down his cutlass and surrenders.

I also had turned yellow and went belly-up. I was a burnt-out charter skipper.

But failure and belly-up are definitely not part of the formula for Dyke and Inga Wilmerding, who for over ten years have operated either their fine old sixty-two-foot Alden schooner *Mandoo* or their new fifty-three-foot ketch *Zulu Warrior* as one of the top charter boats in the Virgin Islands. Years ago, when I limped into St. Thomas a bit battered and bleeding after a long trek from San Diego, the Wilmerdings took me under their wing and provided physical and mental nourishment so that I could compete with them in the charter business. But I was never any kind of competition to these people! Although they are just about always on the go (averaging twenty-five to thirty charter weeks a year), they are never too busy to welcome or help a wandering sailor; there is always room for one or two more at their happy and bountiful supper table, no matter what the circumstances. They seem to thrive on a constant parade of new faces. For this remarkable couple, the charter life is fun, challenging, and satisfying, and their disease is highly contagious to both new guests and old friends. Like a Virgin Islands Statue of Liberty—"give us your tired, your sick, your nervous, your weary"—the Wilmerdings take these up-tight strangers into their cruising home, and after a week or so they are magically transformed into happy, relaxed, and re-juiced friends.

"It may not turn out this way 100 percent of the time," Inga told me once, "but it happens often enough to be really worthwhile. And the big bonus is those months of our own to work on the boat leisurely, cruise to a different area, or whatever's fair . . . drop-out time!"

To my way of thinking, the Wilmerdings represent a unique compromise in successfully blending chartering with the good life of cruising. They share themselves with all comers honestly and naturally like few others I've ever known; they don't know the meaning of the word *stranger*. They will probably be quite embarrassed when they read this story. But I'm just telling it like it is.

SAINTES FISHING BOAT

59

A Sailboat, a Cricket, a Search for Paradise

I'M NOT EXACTLY sure how the cricket came aboard the *Tumbleweed*. We were anchored in Admiralty Bay, Bequia, and hadn't been tied to a dock in many months. Apparently he sneaked aboard in a box or carton that I had brought from ashore (although I'm usually pretty careful about that because of the bugs and cockroaches). But anyway, one night there he was singing away rather mightily—*chirp, chirp, chirp, chirp, chirp* . . .

Now most boat people get pretty upset about unwanted "guests" or stowaways. So every night for the next week when he'd start chirping (he only vocalized at night), I'd try to search him out. But he was a crafty little devil. I'd think that I had him located for sure in a storage locker or cabinet. Then I'd swiftly open the door to really get him, only to find that the chirping noise was behind me. This would go on until I was tired of sneaking fore and aft in the cabin, vainly searching. It soon became apparent that this cricket was a talented ventriloquist.

I inquired among friends on other boats to get advice on ridding *Tumbleweed* of this intruding insect. No one, it seemed, had ever had a cricket on board his boat; cockroaches, ants, flies, mosquitoes, moths, mice, rats, lizards, beetles—yes—but it looked as if I was the first to have a cricket.

Then one friend offered an interesting piece of information: he claimed that men on the old seventeenth- and eighteenth-century sailing ships considered crickets to be an asset and went to considerable effort to have a dozen or so on board their vessels. There were two important reasons: (1) crickets ate other bugs and kept the ship "clean" (they especially considered cockroaches a delicacy), and (2) crickets on board brought good luck; no decent, well-found sailing vessel would consider going to sea without at least one on board. The buccaneers and pirates were especially keen on this.

After receiving this information, my attitude toward my cricket began to change considerably. Actually, the chirping wasn't disagreeable. I realized that it was a happy, soothing sound that was compatible with other normal night sounds on a forty-year-old wood boat: gentle creaks, squeaks, rattles, and groans; wind in the rigging; lapping water on the hull; faint shore sounds of chickens, dogs, and people. I'm afraid I have to admit that I began talking to my cricket occasionally, and it was soon apparent that he needed a name. So "Chipper" was signed on board the *Tumbleweed*.

It was also soon apparent that those sailors of old certainly knew their business about crickets' eating habits. The few roaches on the boat were soon completely eradicated. In fact, I became a bit worried about Chipper's getting enough to eat. So I made sure to leave a few crumbs on the galley counter every night and a tad of clean water in the bottom of the sink.

And good things began happening regularly on the boat. No bountiful strokes of great fortune, just a continuing subtle run of nice everyday occurrences: pleasant sailing with steady, easy winds, smooth and friendly seas, very few violent rain squalls (and when they did hit us, we were ready for them), no equipment failures, no anchor dragging, the little auxiliary engine always starting when it was needed, the galley stove never failing to burn hot and evenly, the toilet never clogging, the weather always fair and dry when paint or varnish was ready to go on. *Tumbleweed* was really a happy ship!

The time came early that summer to leave the Windward-Leeward Islands and explore the western Caribbean. It would be a 1,500-mile downwind passage from the island of Bequia to our initial destination of Isla Providencia—trade wind sailing at its best! *Tumbleweed* was prepared for the cruise, provisions loaded aboard, and a few unneeded items moved ashore to be stored for a while.

Departure morning turned out to be wet and squally, the first bad day in many weeks. The engine balked with a little temper tantrum but finally started. The anchor turned out to be fouled on some junk on the bottom but finally broke loose after more than an hour's work. In raising the twin staysail running rig, one pole broke loose and tore a big hole in the new dacron sail; the other end clobbered me on the shoulder, giving a painful bruise. The sea was rough and confused, and there was lots of rolling, with green water breaking into the cockpit. That evening, the stove burners plugged up in the middle of cooking supper.

You've guessed it, of course. Chipper wasn't on board. He'd jumped ship—accidentally, I hope. There was no chirping that night or any other night.

It was an unpleasant passage. What should have been a great ten-day sailing run in the usually stable trades turned out to be twenty-five days of calms, squalls, and head winds. Nothing really bad happened, but then nothing particularly good happened either, except for finally arriving at Isla Providencia, our new paradise, weary and somewhat battered.

Providencia, ordinarily green and lush, was parched dry; it was going into the third year of a bad drought. The gardens and fruit trees were dead; the cattle were just skin and bones. The farmers and fishermen of Providencia have a reputation for being friendly, poor, and proud, and normally very happy with their simple, peaceful life. But the long drought was having mental as well as physical effects.

Several weeks went by and the situation on the *Tumbleweed* grew even worse, including my getting a series of bad infections on my legs and feet. And then the final blow: One evening I opened a galley locker door and out leaped a giant cockroach—almost the size of my hand. I was sure that he had gone for my throat, but fortunately he missed! It was definitely a dreaded "killer cockroach"!

A few days later I stopped by to see my friend Winston Robinson and inquire about buying several dozen eggs. His chickens had been laying poorly due to a shortage of feed on the island. He sadly informed me that there still were no eggs to sell. As I left, Mrs. Robinson handed me a little paper bag (every so often she had been giving me a few of her baked goodies). Back on the boat, I opened the bag and found some cookies, cornbread—and three small eggs carefully wrapped in tissue paper.

But then in the twilight of the cabin, what seemed to be a very healthy cockroach leaped out of the bottom of Mrs. Robinson's bag and scurried for safety. I narrowly missed him by half an inch with a sharp hand swat.

Later that evening as I was contemplating my declining situation, an old familiar noise sounded from the forward part of the boat. Yep, it was a cricket chirping—another Chipper was back! And I had nearly welcomed him aboard with a death blow!

In the next two weeks there was a renaissance aboard the boat and good things began to happen again. My physical wounds started healing quickly and I was finally able to start making repairs to the boat. It wasn't long before everything was operating again at 100 percent. And that hungry little singing cannibal in short order wiped out all of the roach colony—including "Big Mamoo"!

And then—you won't believe this, but I swear that it really happened —the rains came. Not short little vicious squalls, but long, drenching ground-soakers and cistern-fillers. Soon the island began to get green again, and once more singing and laughing and giggling was heard from the village and the hillsides and the little fishing boats—and from *Tumbleweed*.

Chirp, chirp, chirp, chirp, chirp, chirp . . .

A Long Weather Leg

EACH YEAR NUMEROUS cruising boats leave the west coast of the United States headed south to Mexico and points beyond. Many of them have the West Indies in mind as their pot of gold at the end of the rainbow.

Only a small handful ever make it all the way. Some start dropping by the wayside before they even reach Mexico. They drop out for all the reasons that shatter cruising dreams: lack of experience, the wrong boat, financial troubles, crew problems, sickness. Most of these failures can be lumped under one classification—inadequate planning.

But calling these aborted cruises "failures" is not right, because most are not really fiascoes but rather honest realizations that the "dream adventure" was not turning out to be as pleasant an experience as had been anticipated. To keep trying for a goal that no longer has much value is just being bull-headed.

So would "planning" guarantee success? Of course not; it just puts the odds more in your favor. And overplanning is just as bad as—maybe worse than—underplanning. Overplanners include the would-be cruisers who spend years tied to a dock getting ready for the big voyage: the boat is loaded with gear and equipment; there are backups for the backups; the bilge is filled with canned goods carefully dipped in wax, indelibly marked, and properly cataloged. When they cast off those lines, they'll be ready. Except they'll probably never cast off the lines, because they'll never be quite ready. They're shooting for 100 percent, and that's not very practical for most of us.

Planning and preparation, both physical and mental, involve a compromise that will vary with each individual. Priority requirements must be met. But at some time you reach a point when it's best to crumple up the list, cast off the lines, and go.

The final bubble-buster on this dream cruise to the West Indies is Panama. Here you turn the corner and leave the relatively peaceful, friendly Pacific and start playing games with the boisterous Caribbean. That long weather leg from Panama to the Virgin Islands is usually a brand new ball game.

There's a guy (let's call him Sam) who lives and works in the Canal Zone and makes a tidy sum every year buying cruising boats for about ten cents on the dollar. His method of operation is usually something like this: Sam makes a friendly contact with a new arrival at Balboa on the Pacific side. He spots the boats immediately that are having problems and maybe even helps them make the canal transit to Cristobal on the Caribbean side. Sometimes he even makes a rather low offer for the boat, expecting it to be turned down, but he has established his "base" price.

Sam waves goodbye as they leave the Cristobal breakwater, then waits patiently for about three to seven days, feeling relatively sure that they'll be back—battered and broken and probably beaten.

And too often he's right. He catchs them at the depths of disappointment, despair, and disillusionment. The Caribbean can be a giant mixmaster sea with square waves. And it's 3,500 long uphill miles back to California. Sam makes another offer for the boat, usually quite a bit lower than his original "base" offer. If his timing is right, Sam gets the boat for a ridiculously low price, and the despondent former owners end up with not much more than plane tickets back to the States.

What is this big deal about the "killer" Caribbean? Is it really that bad and disagreeable?

No, but it certainly commands respect—and some planning. The northeast trades are usually blowing and the seas can be rough, especially along coasts where currents can antagonize these wind-generated seas. Ordinarily there is a "good" tack and a "bad" tack; and usually the good tack is the least favorable one relative to your desired course.

This long weather leg can perhaps be best described under three categories: Boat, Route, and Weather.

Boat. The boat has to be ready and able for some brisk, wet sailing. Rigging, gear, sail, and hull (and crew) have to be in good condition.

The boat must have watertight hatches and ports. Healthy working sails will usually be all you need, and the main will probably have a reef tucked in it at least part of the time. A small husky jib (about 60 percent or so of the working jib) would be a real asset. Often it's not the wind strength that dictates the amount of sail area being carried, but rather the short, steep seas. Sometimes you need to slow the boat down to keep from pounding everything and everybody to pieces.

This is definitely a sailing passage. If the boat won't sail reasonably well to weather, then you have a serious problem. If you are planning to do it by mostly motor-sailing, then be prepared for a disagreeable ordeal.

Route. There seem to be three basic routes (plus variations) from Panama to the Virgin Islands (about 1,200 miles rhumb line), assuming that the Virgins are your initial destination in the West Indies. All three have advantages and disadvantages, so the choice becomes largely a personal one dictated by desired stops along the way and available time.

One route would be up the western Caribbean through the Yucatán Channel, over to Florida, then to the Virgins and beyond. If you'd like to go to Florida anyway and cruise the Bahamas, then this route would be fine. Part of the trip to Florida should be on some kind of reach, and there'd be some help part of the way from the Gulf Stream current. And the western Caribbean has some interesting islands that are certainly worth visiting—San Andrés, Providencia, Grand Cayman. The only trouble is that it's about 1,200 miles from Panama to Florida, and then it's another 1,200 miles on to the Virgins—straight to weather as the winds in the southwest North Atlantic tend to be east and southeast. And along much of this route are unlighted reef and shoal areas. Also, if you're a bit unlucky with the weather, the reach part could turn into a beat into a Gulf norther.

The second route would take you to Jamaica. On the starboard tack, hard on the wind, you should be able to lay it. Then it's Jamaica to the Virgins, dead to weather, south of Hispaniola and Puerto Rico.

Taking the third route, you would make your easting up the north coast of Colombia, stopping at Cartagena, Santa Marta, and other anchorages, to Aruba. Then from Aruba you would head for the Virgins on a long starboard tack. If you're lucky and the trades are a little south of east, you could lay the Virgins. The big disadvantage to this route is that strong currents sometimes sweep along portions of the north coast of South America. Also on the negative side is the unfortunate fact that some of the Colombian ports can be dens of thieves, and you must take precautions to prevent serious losses.

Of course you can also sail from Panama to the Virgins with no stops. I know of several boats that have done it this way and have had good passages, favoring whatever tack kept them reasonably close to the rhumb line.

Weather. If you like to outguess the weather or play averages, then the statistics indicate that there are good and not so good times to make the passage. Late April, May, and early June, then late October, November, and early December seem to be the best times if you have a choice. The weather should be more stable and the trades not so fierce. The winter months usually bring stronger winds and rougher seas. July and early August can be boisterous with the reinforced summer trades. July, August, September, and October are potential hurricane months. But to one way of thinking September is the best month of all to make the crossing; the trades should be lighter and the seas easier. Just keep an ear to the radio for any weather developments. Probably a good engine with long fuel range would make September more desirable. And a couple of trusty good luck charms.

Good weather reports for the Caribbean and the Gulf of Mexico are available on a shortwave receiver by monitoring WOM Hi-Seas Radio, Miami, every six hours at 0500, 1100, 1700, and 2300 GMT. I have the best luck receiving the following WOM frequencies: 4.429, 8.793, 13.155, and 17.280 mc. Swan Island Radio in the northwest Caribbean also puts out a detailed weather report daily at 1705 GMT covering the western Caribbean and Gulf on the marine band at 2738 kc. Local stations on the broadcast band also can provide good weather inputs at various times during the day, such as Barbados at 900 kc and Tortola at 780 kc, both of which are 10,000 watts and English-speaking.

So don't become another one of Sam's victims. That "long weather leg" doesn't have to be an ordeal. Rather with a bit of planning, it can be a great adventure. It may be wet and bouncy, but the water's warm! And believe me, the West Indies are worth it all.

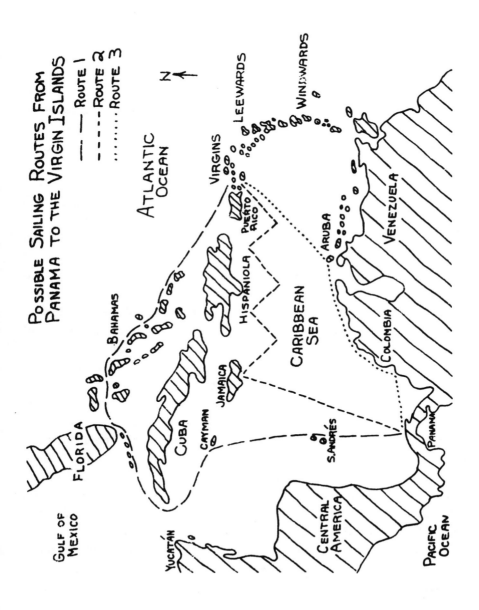

Isla de San Andrés

WAY OUT IN the middle of the western Caribbean are two remote flyspeck islands, San Andrés and Providencia. They are unlike each other except that they both belong to Colombia (although they are five hundred miles from the South American coast).

San Andrés is a coral island, dry and low but very attractive. It is seven miles long by two miles wide, with a population of about 20,000 humans and 500,000 coconut palms. The islanders are friendly, with a pleasant, slow-paced West Indian culture handed down from Jamaican slaves and seventeenth-century buccaneers and seasoned with a vibrant Latin American beat. Although Spanish is the official language, the natural island tongue is an English patois.

Coconuts were about the only source of income until the early 1960s, when the Colombian government made San Andrés a free port and built a modern airport. Now, a half dozen or more flights a day from Central and South American countries bring visitors to stock up on duty-free merchandise imported from all over the world.

As an added attraction, these visitors can relax in the sun and enjoy fine beaches and excellent snorkeling on offshore reefs. For land explorers, the sightseeing is pretty much do-it-yourself via rental bicycles, motorbikes, and mini-jeeps.

For a cruising boat, the best anchorage is at the upper end of the island, to the north and a little east of Cotton Cay. Eyeball navigation will find you a good spot in this area in eight to twenty-five feet of water. The bottom is good holding and you get excellent protection from the big offshore reef to the east and south and from the island to the north and west. A breeze nearly always blows, and you will seldom be bothered by bugs.

On the beach near this anchorage are several good landing spots for the dinghy. "Town" is just a block or so away and a reasonably good supply of staples can usually be found at several *super mercados* and little "mom and pop" stores. A longer walk will take you to a side street with two bakeries, several meat markets, and sometimes fresh produce. Fruits and vegetables are a bit expensive, as they come by plane from Costa Rica.

At this stage of development, San Andrés is still relatively simple and fun. For the Colombians, it's "Hawaii." The facilities and action are kind of rinky-dink and maybe a little primitive. But if you like offbeat places, it's a pleasant, delightful rinky-dinkism. Most of the activity is in the northeast corner of the sland. The business district is a bustling frontier-type area of small stores, street vendors, and sidewalk cafes. A hundred or so little shops bulge with trading-stamp type merchandise. One rather interesting and fast-selling item is a combination TV, AM-FM radio, record player, tape deck, cigarette lighter, and digital clock with snooze alarm—all this in the shape of an outboard motor—with the lower end a Waring blender.

Compared to the islands in the eastern Caribbean, San Andrés is relatively inexpensive by U.S. standards. A room with two meals at one of the better hotels costs about half what you would spend at most West Indian resorts. And adequate accommodations in some of the smaller hotels are even better bargains.

But don't expect to find any semblance of luxury. One visitor has offered this apt description: "Our hotel resembled a colony of rundown pre-World II wooden tourist cabins. There was no hot water. The toilet seat was broken. A dead cockroach decorated the shower. But we decided we hadn't come all that distance for good plumbing. There was plenty of amiable help, an excellent restaurant, and a superb location on a point of land facing out across a lagoon. We could see and hear the surf smashing half a mile away on the offshore reef that shelters the northern and eastern sides of the island. Glistening under a bright sun in the calm turquoise water of the lagoon were several little cays that look like a paradise of white sand and palms."

Aside from coconuts, very little is grown on the island, so just about all food comes from the mainland by ship and plane. But despite shortages, you can eat well at reasonable prices at many of the unpretentious

71

little restaurants that line the beachfront. Most offer delicious fresh seafood dishes such as conch chowder, broiled lobster, and snapper fried in coconut oil.

Like most small Caribbean islands, San Andrés is short of fresh water. Rain-caught cistern water is augmented by slightly brackish well water, but it's scarce, and tap water often flows only a few hours a day.

Cappy Salizar is a Colombian who migrated to San Andrés about fifteen years ago. He has been involved in many different small-scale ventures, none of which has made any money. But he has lots of fun and enjoys an easygoing, low-tempo life. His most recent project has been transforming an abandoned barge into a little waterfront bar-restaurant. Cappy loves San Andrés, but is not at all happy with the mushrooming tourism. "All the big money is being made by outsiders. The average islander is worse off with all this activity. His wages remain low, but he has to buy at tourist-inflated prices. His simple, slow-paced life of past years is fast disappearing. And the undesirables from the mainland are moving in on the action—thieves, banditos, hustlers, and con artists."

As might be expected, there is a lot of speculation in land on the little island, and property prices have skyrocketed. A couple of American hotshots are wheeling and dealing with U.S. visitors who want to make a "smart little investment in paradise." These two characters are very unpopular locally and certainly don't help the Yankee image. But they manage to continue operating with *mordita*—payoffs—to the right people. Property ownership by an alien is rather complicated and title is doubtful. By Latin American standards, the Colombian government is relatively stable, but local officials receive low salaries, and *mordita* is a standard practice when one wants to get anything done, legally or otherwise. So what's new?

San Andrés is booming fast and beginning to show the negative signs of uncontrolled large-scale commercial tourism. More and bigger planes are arriving; a new once-a-week nonstop flight from Miami undoubtedly will be expanded to tap the potentially lucrative U.S. market. San Andrés is being touted as Colombia's low-cost, unspoiled Caribbean paradise that nobody knows about. Just how "undiscovered" can a place be with eight jets a day unloading visitors?

But sixty miles to the north is Isla Providencia, and there you'll find a completely different situation.

Killer Reef Ahead!

IT WAS A glorious morning, sailing at its very best. We were flying the working genny and mizzen staysail, with the wind blowing about twenty knots from the starboard quarter. Seas were moderately rough, but they were behind us, and *Tumbleweed* was scooting along in grand style. We were twenty-five days out of Bequia, bound for Isla Providencia, 1,500 miles downwind and our new "paradise" island in the western Caribbean.

It had been a rather unpleasant passage for the first twenty-three days. But the wind and sea gods at last took mercy on us, and the previous two days had provided daily runs averaging 160 miles. Finally we were getting our storybook sailing.

But on this special morning I was a little edgy, perhaps a normal trait for a navigator on a small boat offshore. It was "landfall time." At around noon Providencia should appear on the horizon to the west. Although it's only a small island, six miles long by three miles wide, Providencia is relatively high, 1,500 feet at its highest peaks and ridges. The east coast is ringed by an offshore barrier reef that extends ten miles to the north and west of the island. With reasonably good visibility, we should be able to pick up Providencia about twenty miles out.

So there should be no worry with an easy landfall coming up at high noon with almost perfect weather.

But I was wondering a bit about my navigation. My sextant for this passage was a little $12.95 plastic instrument. Unfortunately, just a few days before we left Bequia my good old Plath had been stolen. The plastic job had been on board for several years as an emergency backup sextant; now it was called into first-line duty.

I checked it out thoroughly prior to departure with a number of sun sights and was reasonably confident that it could get us to Prov-

73

idencia. Twilight star shots were not very practical because there were no optical lenses in the sighting tube.

In actual use, the only real problem was a highly variable index error. Being just lightweight plastic, the change from the cooler shady cabin to the warmer sunny deck produced a temperature change warpage that sometimes gave an instrument error of more than fifteen minutes, certainly a negative factor for trying to achieve reasonable accuracy.

So I followed the simple procedure of allowing the sextant to "stabilize" in the sun prior to each use. Adjustments would then be made if necessary and an index error determined. Immediately after the sight was taken, a final index error was noted, and if it was within a minute or so of the intial error, then the shot was considered to be good.

As the days went by, I had no reason to doubt the measurements of this cheap little sextant. The sun line fixes were fairly close to the dead reckoning positions.

There were no offshore dangers until we were in the vicinity of Providencia; then things could get a little tight. About seventy-five miles east of the island is an extensive shoal area called Roncador Bank; sixty miles to the northeast is the large reef development of Serrana. And forty miles to the north and south of the island are the dangerous shoals of Quita Sueno and Cayos del Este. No dependable navigational lights mark any of these reefs, and strong currents sweep through this portion of the sea. The fine old racing schooner *Morning Star* was lost in this area on a squally night in 1966.

Our planned course was to take us midway between Roncador and Serrana, giving a safety margin of some fifteen miles on each side. My 9:00 A.M. sun line and DR position indicated that we were safely through the "pass" and about twenty miles east of Providencia. We carefully searched the horizon but saw only sun-flecked sea and bright sky.

By 11:00 A.M. I was concerned; Providencia should be about five miles away, but the horizon was still empty.

At 11:15 the bow watch hollered, "Reef ahead!" And what a reef it was! From out of nowhere a wild series of roaring breakers and cascading froth extended to port and starboard as far as we could see.

We immediately came up on a beam reach heading north. I rushed below and hurriedly checked the charts, but I had no indication of which reef area we had found. And then the breakers ended, with deep water to the north and west. We turned downwind again and ran down the upper side; inside the reef to the south were shallow, beautifully colored water and several low, sandy cays. After several miles the reef ended, leaving deep water to the south, so we jibed over and reached in that direction, carefully eyeballing our course and looking for a spot to anchor.

Where in the hell were we? What had gone wrong with my navigation? That damn piece of plastic junk had really led us astray. I kicked myself for being so careless. But what a lucky break that we'd found this reef during daylight!

I climbed the ratlines to the lower spreaders to pick out a reasonable anchorage here in the middle of nowhere. And then to the south appeared the faint outline of peaks and ridges!

It was Providencia, only about five miles away! I had seriously misjudged the visibility, not realizing that a heavy salt haze in the air had obscured the island until we were almost on top of it.

Safely anchored that night in Catalina Harbor off little Isabel Village, we enjoyed much laughing and giggling and tinkling of glasses. I carefully cleaned my little $12.95 Tupperware sextant, gently stored it away, and silently apologized for questioning its capability.

There was no doubt as to who was the weak link in the chain.

Isla Providencia

ISLA PROVIDENCIA STANDS almost alone in the vast emptiness of the western Caribbean Sea. It is a volcanic island of fertile green hills and flowered valleys, a beautiful confusion of peaks, domes, and cliffs. As you come in from the sea, a faint fragrance of orange blossoms drifts out to meet you.

It is also an island that time and man seem to have long forgotten.

Centuries ago Providencia was coveted for its strategic location in the heart of the trade routes of Spanish galleons sailing back to Europe heavily laden with New World riches. Today the island is a cultural museum where the simple and leisurely way of life of an earlier era has been isolated and preserved.

It is the home of some three thousand farmers and fishermen, descendants of English, Spanish, Dutch, Portuguese, and French adventurers and colonialists. The strongest contingent to hold the island were seventeenth- and eighteenth-century pirates and buccaneers, including Henry Morgan, William Bligh, and Luis Aury. History strongly suggests that much of the treasure that Morgan carried off when he sacked Panama City was hidden away on Providencia. The natives have an inexhaustible number of theories regarding where this treasure might be buried. Most think it is off the northwest coast in a secret underwater cave. More than one visitor has discreetly bought an "authentic" treasure map from old Cap'n John, the island con man.

A long history of intermingling of the races provides a population best described by an islander: "Some is white and some is black, but most's da color o' chawed tobacky."

Catalina Harbor on the northwest coast provides a fine, smooth anchorage in eight to ten feet of water off Isabel Village, well protected by the main island to the east and south, the smaller island of Catalina to the north, and by an extensive reef to the west. Entering the bay through one of the several passes in the reef should be done only in good light. An offshore barrier reef on the east side of the island extends ten miles to the north and west, forming a fifteen thousand-acre area offering some of the finest diving in the Caribbean.

A road of sorts circles the island. Although islanders have a dozen or so pickup trucks, the chief means of transportation are horses and small boats powered by sail or oars. In the event of important news, a "town crier" circles the island on horseback, stopping at intervals to shout the announcement. Limited supplies are brought to the island by the *Arcabra*, a modern version of Noah's Ark, which makes a round trip between Panama and Providencia (by way of San Andrés) about every three weeks or so. The boat's arrival at the island is always a holiday.

Several years ago a small landing strip was completed, and a little twin-engine Beechcraft began air service from San Andrés, sixty miles to the south. Supposedly, two round-trip flights are scheduled per day. But some problem usually develops with the plane or the pilot or the weather, so air service ranges from erratic to nonexistent.

Isabel Village is the main community. A half dozen little stores provide basics such as flour, rice, sugar, and salt, but the islanders are relatively self-sufficient, raising individual gardens, fruit trees, livestock, and fish. Isabel Village has no central market, so one must know who grows bananas and papayas, who will sell or trade a few eggs or oranges, who might be baking extra bread. When a fisherman arrives on the beach with his catch whoever needs fish runs down for first choice. Grouper and snapper are very inexpensive. Lobster is plentiful, but the islanders can't afford such luxury eating, as this delicacy is sold for relatively high prices to the San Andrés tourist market.

A local resident explained why Providencia doesn't have a central market, "These people are very proud. If one of them has a good mango tree, he wants his neighbor to come to him for mangoes." To have something to sell or trade and to be sought out seems important to the islanders.

Recently, a government-financed fourteen-room hotel was completed in anticipation of a tourist "boom." But few visitors have made their way to this quiet island—it's very difficult and inconvenient to reach. One traveler had the following comments, "Serving as a terminal for the dirt airstrip is a weather-beaten shack. The airport limousine is an open truck with wooden benches. At the hotel, oil drums were stored in the lobby, which was also the island post office. The man who assembled our bathroom had evidently never used one. The shower delivered about enough water to dampen a toothbrush. The next day the water stopped running altogether."

I remember a brief conversation with a heavy-set, hard-drinking Texan who was on the island for a short time, apparently scouting for bargain property. He said he represented a big Houston land syndicate and confided, "These savages don't want to sell."

By U.S. standards the islanders' living would be considered bare existence. But nature has endowed their little island with the essentials. The sea and the land provide fish, fruits, and vegetables. Cattle graze the hillsides, and every family has chickens and usually a few pigs. Still, it is an impoverished island in the sense of a modern money economy. The small earnings of the men who go to sea or to the mainland and the sales of livestock and fish to San Andrés are about the only sources of income. The few things that the islanders buy from the outside world are outrageously priced.

The island is ruled by outcast and disinterested Colombian government officials who apparently view their assignment to Providencia as somewhat comparable to a prison sentence to Devil's Island.

Today, although luxury cruise ships and large freighters pass within sight of the island and giant jet airliners streaking to Florida or Panama are dimly visible overhead almost every day, Providencia is perhaps more isolated than it was two centuries ago. Although anxious for better communications with the outside world, many of the islanders fear that more contact could seriously damage their leisurely way of life. They have witnessed the rape of their neighbor to the south, San Andrés. They hear serious rumors that the Colombian government plans to make Providencia an exclusive hideaway for wealthy politicians and industrialists.

But even though "progress" threatens, the Providencians are a strong people with a hardy background and will fight hard to retain the values of their peaceful community. They awaken each morning to the crowing of roosters and go to sleep every night to the singing of crickets.

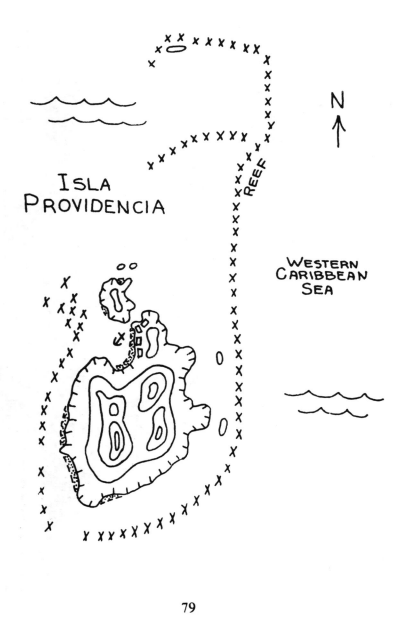

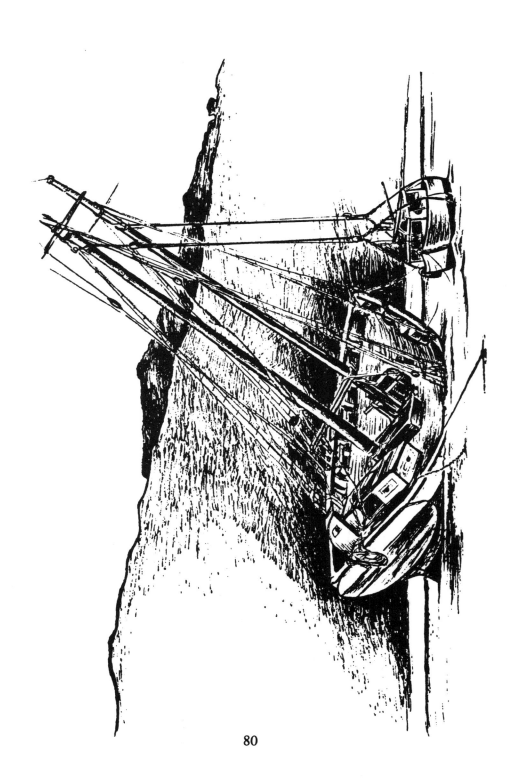

Yachties

*YACHTIE (colloquial): A vagabond sailor
who lives by his wits.*

HE'S A MAVERICK gypsy of the high seas who roams around in a sailboat, sometimes a vintage creation that's a bit in disrepair (but usually
relatively seaworthy) or maybe a backyard ensemble that he's put together himself. He will stay in port just long enough to scrape together
sufficient money to make another passage searching for a new paradise.
Although harbor authorities may sometimes ask him to leave before he
is quite ready, that seems to be a small price to pay for his independence
and freedom. But the yachtie isn't necessarily an escapist, nor is he angry
or disillusioned or thumbing his nose at the establishment; he's just
quietly doing his own thing, practicing the simple positive philosophy
that "today just might be the best day of my life." And there is a very
distinct difference between a bum and a tramp. A bum has no purpose
in life; a tramp has one—he is determined not to become a bum.

A *yachtie* is not to be confused with a *yachtsman* or a *racer* or a
cruiser; these are all distinctly different breeds of serious offshore boat
people. All seem to enjoy their own particular manner and style of boat-
ing thoroughly—and sometimes are even known to socialize (very discreetly) with one another.

You'll usually find the yachtsman tied to the dock at a plush
marina or club, like Faro Blanco at Marathon, Ocean Reef on Key
Largo, Pier 66 in Fort Lauderdale, Old Port Cove in Palm Beach. His
vessel is large, gleaming, and resplendent with chrome, varnish, leather,
teak, and elegance; it is immaculately maintained by a uniformed
captain and crew. You can just about always spot a thoroughbred
yachtsman by his blue blazer, shiny brass buttons, and hand-tooled

unborn buffalo-skin deck shoes. A true yachtsman will usually have a svelte bikini-clad personal secretary on board, and a jaunty, just-groomed, beribboned poodle perched on the foredeck. The yachtsman spends a lot of time in the club bar trading sea stories—and stock market tips.

The racer is an inveterate, gung-ho, go-fast sailor, and racing is the only thing that has any real importance in his life. Everything else is secondary or of very little value; competing and winning is what it's all about. His boat is a bewildering maze of winches, blocks, sheets, halyards, bags of sails, whirring and clicking electronic goodies—anything that can possibly milk an extra ounce of power out of the wind gods. It is an unquenchable sponge that sucks up every dollar that he can beg, borrow, or steal; he thinks nothing of spending $100,000 to try for one twenty-five-dollar silver-plated plaque. A true racer will quit a high-salaried job, divorce a loyal wife, and sell his daughter into slavery if they jeopardize, conflict with, or in any way restrict his racing activities.

The cruiser can also be found tied to the dock, but the marina surroundings are much more modest: Boot Key in Marathon, Anchor Inn at Miami, Riverbend in Fort Lauderdale, Dan's Docks in West Palm. His boat is usually kept in excellent condition, but it noticeably lacks the size and spit and polish of that of the yachtsman or the ultimate sailing qualities of that of the racer. Often the boat is a stock fiberglass model; the cruiser believes that this represents the most practical type of vessel for trouble-free voyaging. But he makes many modifications such as converting bunks to storage, doubling the fuel capacity for the auxiliary engine, beefing up the rigging. He also adds (over a period of time) several truckloads of gear and equipment such as cockpit windshield and dodgers, survival life rafts, assorted sea anchors, storm trysails, speedometers, fathometers, wind indicators with flashing dials and digital readouts, refrigeration, a half-dozen or so radios, and a high-intensity one million candlepower masthead strobe light.

The bilges and lockers are crammed with hundreds of cans of Spam, Dinty Moore stew, chili con carne, Campbell's soup, Beef-A-Roni, and Beanie-Weenies—all carefully dipped in wax. The really serious cruiser will just about always have a two-thousand-dollar Hasler or

QXV Mark IV self-steering wind-vane gear swinging around off the stern of his boat. Even if he never uses it or can never make it work, it's still well worth the investment. Its presence marks him as a true offshore passage-maker; he has the respect and envy of the entire dock.

The cruiser is always getting ready for the Big Cruise. He is also a legitimate member of society; both he and his wife probably have good jobs. His cruising is done in organized increments, maybe a week, a month, or a year. Then he goes back to a job to get ready for the next chapter. The cruiser is the real scientist of sailing, the hard-working, constructive "doer." He's a planner, a coordinator, a designer, a builder, a thinker.

But this story started out about yachties. What are they really like? What's their class description?

By his very nature, the yachtie can't be categorized. He is truly a free spirit. He firmly—almost violently—resists classification and finds being called a "yachtie" most distasteful. Rather than being a loner, he is a private person, usually a low-profile type. He asks for no handouts or welfare; he is very proud and makes his own way in a simple manner. He will very seldom be tied to a dock, much preferring to be anchored in an out-of-the-way spot. A yachtie's boat is usually adequate and reasonably comfortable, but it has very few frills or goody items. The yachtie sails the offbeat seas without a thought of help from the outside, satisfied that should he meet trouble he will be able to handle it. And if he can't—well, that's the life he chose. He doesn't believe in taking foolish chances, but he knows that there is very seldom anything really worthwhile that can be accomplished without taking any chances at all.

His abilities can represent a wide range of versatility; he might be an engineer, a mechanic, a carpenter, an electrician, an artist. When he needs money, he puts his skills to work, but for no longer than it takes to get a traveling stake together. His personal freedom and time are precious commodities that have no dollar value. He is a slave only to himself. Security is no problem because he has confidence and optimism and curiosity and imagination. A true yachtie believes that a rut is only another name for a grave, and that the only way to stay out of ruts is by living adventurously in a search for personal truths and staying vitally alive every day of his life. Sometimes he may find it necessary to wash dishes or sweep streets or collect garbage, but that doesn't bother him because he knows that very soon he will once again be able to soar with the eagles and hoot with the owls.

In contrast to the yachtie, the cruiser is usually very well organized and takes pride in keeping a relatively tight schedule. If his plans call for arriving in Acapulco on August 14 at 3:00 P.M., he means it and will probably be right on time. The yachtie, on the other hand, is not even sure that he'll stop in Acapulco; if so, he says it might be late summer, or in the winter, or maybe next spring—whatever's fair. The yachtie isn't exactly disorganized; he's just loose and flexible. And free.

Cruisers and yachties usually like music. The cruiser will probably have a five-hundred-dollar stereo tape system; the yachtie will have a beat-up twenty-five-dollar guitar. The cruiser will usually have a powerful auxiliary diesel engine to help him make fast passages and keep the schedule and to maneuver into marina docks. The yachtie may or may not have an engine. If he has one, and if it happens to run, it usually is used only for getting in and out of tricky anchorages. If light winds provide a slow passage, then so be it; he's in no hurry. Sailing his boat is a most pleasant experience.

A few yachties attain notoriety, and they're the ones that you hear about. There's René, a Dane who spent a number of years roaming the West Indies. He was a handsome rascal, with bronzed, sinewy muscles, long flaxen locks, and a small gold ring in his left ear. His method of survival was cultivating well-to-do and well-endowed females—he was known among his acquaintances as "Prince Gallant." His ultimate coup came in St. Thomas. A long unlucky streak made it necessary for relatives in Europe to send him a modest advance of about $150. The money transfer was handled by the local branch of the Bank of America. But a slight error was made in converting the transferred Danish kroner into U.S. dollars, and he received $8,500. That night Prince Gallant threw a never-to-be-forgotten wingding on the old docks at Yacht Haven that put a sizable dent in his new bankroll. Just before dawn, he sailed out of the harbor bound for parts unknown—accompanied by the pretty bank teller who had handled his recent transaction.

And then there was the infamous Mabel. One of the many incidents involving her occurred in the British Virgin Islands at the Royal Tortola

Yacht Club. Henry, the bartender in the stag bar, has given the following account and swears that it is true. The trouble began, Henry says, when the captain and crew of a recently arrived small yacht dropped in one evening for a few drinks. Because of the nature of the bar, it was permissible to serve the male crew but not the captain, who was a hefty woman in her late twenties. Henry politely informed her that she would have to drink her cocktails in the lounge with the rest of the women. Her reply was right to the point, "I am the captain of that goddam boat out there, and if my crew can stand and drink at this bar, so can I."

It happened that most of the men at the bar that night were ocean sailors, and none could find fault with her argument. So the Amazon captain got her rum at the bar. But so often when you relax the rules someone gets hurt. In this case it was a British gentleman standing next to Mabel. The captain, after a few drinks, horrified the group by announcing that she had been too long at sea, disrobed and offered to share herself with all of her new friends. She informed the British gentleman that he could be first. When he declined the invitation, she questioned his manhood. He replied that he might not be a man, but there was no question that she was not a lady. As Henry tells it, Madam Captain sprang to her feet, grabbed a bar stool, and cold-cocked the British gentleman, who was hospitalized for two weeks. Since this incident, says Henry, the stag bar rules have been rigidly enforced.

Many yachties support themselves like the land gypsies of olden times. These modern sea wanderers make and repair and sell, usually unique items representing their personal creativity and finely crafted from canvas, straw, wood, leather, string, or brass. Often, he utilizes a trade or hobby or aptitude that he already knows. Sometimes he learns a new one, which might mean going to an evening trade school or perhaps working as an apprentice. Jake Howard used to peddle used cars, but he spent his last year ashore working for a sailmaker in Fort Lauderdale. Every harbor that he now sails into has potential customers waiting for him. His thirty-six-foot yawl *Footloose* is a miniature sail loft, complete with a little heavy-duty hand sewing machine.

Pete Morris roams the Caribbean using his forty-foot cutter *Easy Street* as his gypsy workshop, his raw materials easily available from beachcombing. One of his specialty items is a wild-looking head fashioned from an old dried-up coconut, with facial features created by utilizing beans, shells, rocks, driftwood, coral, and palm fronds. Each customer gets the following descriptive paper:

I AM A *WHAMBY*

I am very old.
I come from the magic isles of the Caribbees.
Our mysterious and mighty powers have never been equaled.
There are just a few of us, yet one for each of you!
We are always very busy.
We feed the birds and the hermit crabs,
Gather flies and mosquitoes for the spiders.
We supply moonbeams for your hair
Mist for the meadows
And gentle trade wind breezes.
We make babies laugh and little girls pretty,
The stars twinkle and the reefs roar.
We carefully guard the old pirate treasures
And call in the lobster from the deep ocean.
We color the sky blue and the water green and the reefs red
          and yellow.
We paint butterfly wings
And grind up sharp rocks into powder-soft sugar-sand beaches.
We turn the deep forests into fairylands of magnificent beauty
Because that's where our home is!
We move quicker than lightning,
So very few have ever seen us.
We do our job with loving care
And expect you to do the same!
Then we will always take care of you!
And *remember* . . . for your own sake:
Every time a gloomy non-believer says
          "There's no such thing as a WHAMBY!"
. . . Somewhere a little old WHAMBY dies . . .

But I guess maybe my favorite yachtie is Sam Bradley. Not long ago I was anchored off the commercial docks on the west side of Key West, Florida. I glanced up and there was *Rainbow* short-tacking up the channel—a fifty-foot gaff-rigged schooner that looked as if it were over a hundred years old and maybe was. What in the world was good old Cap'n Sam doing sailing into Key West?

Sam's scene was the Caribbean. He had been sailing that beat-up old schooner up and down the West Indies for as long as even the old-timers could remember. And he was usually by himself, although every now and then someone would report seeing a woman on board.

He anchored over by Tony's Fish Market just before sunset. I rowed over in the dinghy, and we spent the evening catching up on the last couple of years.

Some say that Sam used to be a very successful electrical engineer and that he still gets royalties from a few small patent rights—enough to support his wanderings. *Rainbow* doesn't exactly impress you as belonging to a man electrically inclined. There's not a single electrical fixture or piece of wiring on board—just a couple of kerosene lamps. And no engine . . . Sam is really a sailor's sailor.

He was just coming in from the Cayman Islands in the northwest Caribbean, about a six-hundred-mile passage around the west end of Cuba through the Yucatán Channel to Key West.

"Forty days she was," said Sam, "and shouldn't have taken any longer than eight or ten. But seems like everything was against me. Can't remember when I've had such lousy sailing. The wind and sea gods was sure upset about something."

Before Cayman, he'd stopped in Jamaica. "Ran into a weird deal there. A couple of bushy-haired lads wanted to sail to Florida—said they were looking for 'an adventure under a spread of sail'—gave me a thousand bucks for the trip. They came on board with eight big burlap bags stuffed full of what seemed to be just a bunch of funny-smelling leaves. But they called it 'island souvenirs.' Well, we had a wild run to Grand Cayman, just 180 miles, but the old trades were really hootin' and hissin', big seas—curling, cresting, breaking—all that cheap stuff. We parted company one night in Cayman and they left with their eight burlap bags. Said the 'souvenirs' was getting all wet."

But what was Sam doing in Florida? This just wasn't his cup of tea.

"Came up to fetch Cindy. Said she'd go back to the islands with me if I'd come to Florida and get her."

Lordy . . . Cindy Goober. Love really is blind. I remembered her from St. Thomas, and she had to be one of the most unattractive girls I've ever seen—definitely a prime candidate for Miss Moonshot. And talk—she babbled constantly. Sam had left Grenada six months ago and sailed over three thousand miles . . . to fetch Cindy. Wow!

"I know what you're thinkin'," said Sam. "Cindy's not exactly every man's idea of a queen. But I like her a lot; the boat likes her; and we all feel comfortable and happy when she's around."

A pretty basic testimonial.

I squeezed a little personal history out of Sam. "My first real blue-water cruising boat was a fine little Alden ketch named *Windflower*, which I very foolishly sold due to my wife's idea of buying a house and my father's advice to invest in a business. Luckily, before the money was flushed down the drain, I came to my senses, took a freighter to England, and found *Rainbow*. My wife was real upset, threw a big temper tantrum, then gave me an ultimatum: It was either her or the boat. That was the easiest decision I've ever made."

A couple of mornings later, I looked out and the old schooner was gone. I assume Cindy had been fetched and they were headed back to the islands.

Some men spend their lives chasing rainbows. Sam Bradley lives on one.

A total committment to the life style of a sea gypsy is certainly not to everyone's liking. And most fortunately, or otherwise paradise would soon become quite crowded. It's all a very delicate personal balance of values—each person's recipe for the best compromise with life is different—which of course is the way it should be.

The conforming landsman shakes his head and says, "I don't see how you can afford to live this kind of a life."

The maverick yachtie gazes at the distant horizon and replies, "I don't see how I can afford not to."

Yachtsmen sometimes are also racers, and racers oftentimes in their maturing years become cruisers. A few cruisers evolve into yachties.

But I've never known a yachtie who became a yachtsman.

Cayman Islands

BROCHURES AND TRAVEL guides describe them as "the islands that time forgot."

Well, the clock is running again.

Construction cranes tower above the palm trees as new hotels, condominiums, banks, and stores are being built. The waterfront at Georgetown is packed with small freighters and container ships unloading supplies and equipment. Jets are bringing in vacationers and financial speculators. The little roads and village streets are swarming with cars, trucks, and motorcycles.

Grand Cayman is booming.

The three islands of Grand Cayman, Little Cayman, and Cayman Brac are located in the northwest Caribbean Sea about 175 miles northwest of Jamaica and 150 miles south of Cuba. They are low-lying coral islands with coastlines that vary from white sand beaches to rugged cliffs. They are ringed by offshore barrier reefs that form sounds and lagoons.

Grand Cayman, with a population of about twelve thousand, is where it's all happening. The island is twenty-two miles long and averages about five miles in width. On the western shore is the famous Seven Mile Beach, one of the finest in the Caribbean, which stretches from the business community of Georgetown to the village of West Bay.

Cayman Brac is seventy miles northeast of Grand Cayman and is a mile-wide ribbon about twelve miles long. With a small population of around twelve hundred, it is the most scenic of the three islands—a limestone plateau with deserted beaches, cliffs, green pastures, and coconut palms.

Little Cayman is five miles west of Brac. It is nine miles long and has a population of less than fifty. Both of the smaller islands have airstrips with daily small plane service to Grand Cayman.

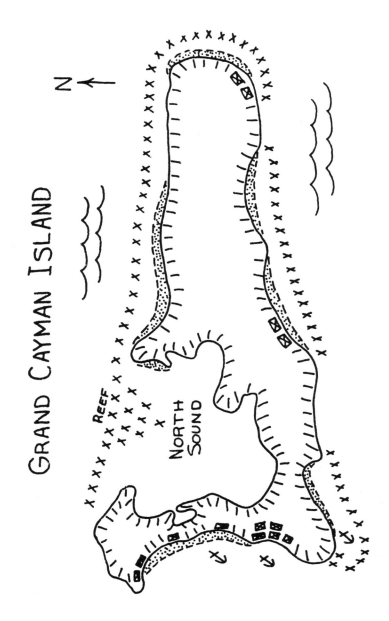

GRAND CAYMAN ISLAND

N

REEF

NORTH
SOUND

For the cruising sailor, good anchorages in the Caymans are scarce. The long west shore of Grand Cayman offers plenty of room and reasonable protection from the normal easterly trade winds. However, it's an open roadstead and tends to roll a bit much of the time. About four to six times each winter a strong "norther" makes its way south from the Gulf of Mexico and can really kick up the western Caribbean with heavy winds and rough seas for thirty-six to seventy-two hours. The west shore anchorage then becomes very dangerous and must be vacated.

My favorite anchorage on Grand Cayman is inside the reef off the southwest tip of the island in an area officially called South Sound but known locally as Buccaneer Cove. Entrance the first time should be with local knowledge and in good light to eyeball yourself through the narrow opening in the reef in about eight feet of water. This is a very pleasant and protected anchorage with great diving less than a hundred feet from the boat.

The early history of Grand Cayman was filled with freebooters, pirates, shipwrecks, and lucrative turtle fishing. The Caymans had one of the largest nesting colonies of green turtles in the world. But by the end of the nineteenth century the turtles were almost extinct because of uncontrolled slaughter and collection of eggs.

Apparently the Caymans were a pirates' paradise. The harbors were well protected by reefs and shoals against intruders, giving the pirates an opportunity to outfit and careen their boats, covering the bottoms with sulfur and tallow for speed and for antifouling protection. The islands also offered fresh water, fish, turtles, and birds for consumption and plentiful hardwoods for ship repairs.

Because they were so low, the islands were hard to see from a distance, and they made an excellent hiding place for buccaneers who lay in wait for Spanish ships on the main trade routes between Central America, Cuba, Jamaica, and Florida. Although the Spanish ships were adequate for their own purposes, they were poorly rigged, slow, and clumsy and were easily overtaken by the fast, close-winded sloops of the English freebooters.

Through the years over three hundred wrecks are known to have occurred on the barrier reefs surrounding Grand Cayman. The most famous was the Wreck of the Ten Sail. One November night in 1788 the *Cordelia*, leading a fleet of merchant vessels bound for England, struck the reef in Gun Bay at the east end of Grand Cayman. A strong northeaster was blowing, and the sailing master had made an error. The *Cordelia* signaled the ships following her to keep off, but her warning was misinterpreted. Each captain thought he was to close up, and all nine other vessels foundered on the reef.

In spite of the rough seas, the nearby villagers made their way out to the reef and helped save the seamen from the wrecks. King George III was so grateful and so impressed by their courage that he granted the Caymanians freedom from conscription in wartime and freedom from any taxation.

In the mid-nineteenth century the Caymans passed from the age of the pirates to a period of continuous settlement and quiet stability. A mixture of Englishmen, Irishmen, Scotsmen, Scandinavians, and former Jamaican slaves—many of whom were survivors from wrecked vessels—found that these little islands offered an adequate livelihood in a balmy climate.

The first hotel, Galleon Beach, was opened on Seven Mile Beach in 1950 and was the forerunner of such small, comfortable inns and guest houses as the Caribbean Club, Beach Club Colony, and Pan Cayman House. On the north and east coasts, the Rum Point Club and Tortuga Club offer their distinctive, informal styles of hospitality. Cayman Brac has its pleasant little Buccaneers' Inn and Skipper's Lodge.

Because of the offshore reefs, the waters are safe, clear, and warm. The visitor can participate in many activities—diving, sailing, and deep-sea fishing, as well as less energetic forms of beachmanship and hammocking. A casual atmosphere has always been the keynote of a Caymanian holiday, and the people are wonderful hosts.

But this uncomplicated, easygoing life style is undergoing a rapid change. In less than ten years, with Miami only a one-hour jet flight away, the number of annual visitors has increased from five thousand to over fifty thousand. The Holiday Inn has established a formidable foothold with a new 185-room beach facility. Frontage on Seven Mile Beach is priced at over two thousand dollars per foot. Cayman has been discovered again.

One of the interesting features of Grand Cayman is its new role as a

92

financial center. At last count 160 banks existed for the twelve thousand people of the island. That comes to one bank for every eighty citizens. Ridiculous!

But it's true. Less than a half dozen banks, however, offer services to the general public. Many of the rest are not much more than "paper" banks and trust companies operating out of two-desk offices. But many are branches or affiliates of legitimate banks and financial institutions from all over the world, including New York, Montreal, Tokyo, London, Paris, Zurich, and Frankfurt.

But why the sudden influx to Grand Cayman?

For many years Americans, Canadians, and Europeans have avoided taxes on some or all of their income by placing money in "offshore" investments, banks, and companies located outside their home countries. Often, this capital is reinvested in U.S. securities, real estate, and commercial developments. And a certain amount of "hot" money always must be hidden away or washed.

Nassau in the Bahamas has long been the headquarters for the operations that deal in this offshore money. But in recent years many of these "numbered account" floating dollars have moved out of the Bahamas to avoid a somewhat unfavorable political and economic climate. Since the Bahamas' full independence from Britain in July 1973, those islands no longer have the full confidence of the international financial operators. Tourist revenues have taken a sizeable drop, and investors show concern over an atmosphere of declining real estate values.

What better place to move than to the Cayman Islands, a British crown colony that has no intention of changing from this favored status? As a tax haven, they are almost perfect, for they have none of the following taxes: income, capital gains, property, sales, corporate, estate, or inheritance. A bank secrecy law protects investors from scrutiny by foreign tax collectors. The government is stable and headed by an appointed British governor general. There seems to be no major friction between British officials and the native-born island administrators.

The banks have set up shop to service over five thousand companies and corporations registered with the local government. Many of these firms operate by buying stocks and securities through brokerage houses in New York, London, and other financial centers. Because they do not have to report the earnings from such investments to the IRS, U.S. shareholders can avoid the taxes that might otherwise be due on them. Businessmen fly in daily to file new company registrations. As long as they comply with a few basic regulations, they are free to run their firms with no government interference. An investment banker has remarked, "We like the place because it is suitably devoid of restrictive laws."

The local government has eagerly accepted the new businessmen. "Oh, sure, some people say being a tax shelter is just a gimmick," says Finance Minister Vassel Johnson, a Caymanian. "But you've got to look at the good side, too. We've got new banks and new hotels and new buildings and jobs for everyone."

Johnson explained further: "It is extremely important that our government remain on the alert for shrewd, manipulating, unsavory operators who are constantly in search of loopholes so as to take unfair and unlawful advantages in our tax-free community. This is a serious ill that has eroded the tax haven systems of other countries. It will ruin ours if we are not careful. It is most important that we provide political stability so as to instill confidence and faith in the future of the Cayman Islands."

There is a new five-story building housing the First National City Bank of New York in the center of Georgetown. Recently, the Bank of Montreal completed a similar structure, and several other banks are building. Unfortunately, most of these new constructions are featureless concrete slabs with little West Indian architectural personality or warmth.

Traffic has become such a problem in the little community that an involved one-way street system had to be put in effect. The new downtown area is alive with serious-looking, brisk men in business suits carrying briefcases rather than relaxed vacationers in bermuda shorts carrying cameras. Developers have plans for more hotels, a protected deep-water harbor, airport expansion, several resort-marina complexes, and a forest of condominiums. The questions of water, power, and sewerage seem to bother very few.

But one man who is deeply concerned is J. M. Bodden, a member of the legislative assembly, who has said, "I doubt that there is any other place in the world with twelve thousand people that has the problems we face here."

Marine life, sea shelves, underwater coral gardens caves, century-old wrecks, spectacular drop-offs—this is the world of Bob Soto, expert diver and explorer of the Caribbean. He has probably done more than any other man to spread the word about the Cayman Islands' prime place in that eighth continent of the world—the underwater.

Born in Cuba of Caymanian and Spanish parents, Soto has lived in the Caymans since the age of three, except for a twelve-year absence while he was a seaman in the Merchant Marine. In 1957 he started his Diving Headquarters and since then has guided thousands of visitors through the underworld beauty of the Cayman Islands. Soto now has one of the largest diving facilities in the world. He can handle two hundred divers a day with a fleet of six boats, full equipment, instruction, and a diving lodge at the eastern end of the island.

The entire Soto family is involved in the operation of the business. His wife, Elita, is the only one who is not a diver, but she stays busy taking care of the shop. Three young sons are following in their father's footsteps; they are good sailors in the Cayman tradition and have been diving since the age of five.

When asked what divers find most interesting in the Caymans, Soto answers, "The clearness of the water and the beautiful development of live reefs with thousands of marine organisms. They just can't believe it when they can see 100 to 150 feet in all directions. And everyone is fascinated by all the wrecks. With over seventy-five miles of shoreline, a lot of it with barrier reefs, the entire island offers the finest diving in the world, especially the east end and Northwest Point.

"But I guess my favorite place is the drop-off on the north coast. When I'm sure that a diver has the proper experience and confidence, this is where I take him for the ultimate in diving accomplishment. The drop-off starts at fifty feet, goes down to six hundred feet, and is honey-combed with fissures and caves. Covering the "wall" are hundreds of colorful varieties of coral, sponges, fans, and fish. Starting at about seventy-five feet, the rare black coral appears. The deeper you drop down the wall, the bigger the forest of black coral becomes. Your body is completely weightless and suspended as you gaze around you."

Soto's biggest thrill is night diving. "There is this strange feeling of a wall of darkness, and then the underwater lights illuminate fish and coral into the most vivid and unbelievable colors, even more outstanding than during the daytime. Strange shapes move in the darkened background. I get a tremendous feeling of eeriness, adventure, and excitement."

Soto is actively involved in the Cayman Islands Conservation Group, which is intent on making sure that this special Cayman treasure will not be lost or destroyed. He wants the beauty of the Cayman waters and islands maintained and is trying to get more Caymanians interested in and concerned about their natural heritage. He's very encouraged to see that many diving visitors have replaced the spear gun with the camera as their chosen underwater weapon. But he's very discouraged by the rapidly increasing commercial activity, large-scale dredging in North Sound, and pollution.

"Caymanians must start doing something now so that future generations will be able to enjoy the privilege of clean waters and live reefs. Our unpolluted water, beaches, and undersea world are our greatest natural resources. If we kill that we will have nothing left."

How much larger will his Diving Headquarters operation get? "I've learned that *big* usually doesn't mean *better*," says Soto. "I wish I could go back about five years and level off at that point. At that stage it was a lot of work and a lot of fun. Now it's just a lot of work. Diving can be very dangerous when not handled properly. There just can't be any compromise with instruction, equipment, or supervision. My biggest problem is getting and keeping the right people to work for me. They have to be top, qualified divers and instructors capable of handling people. And the logistics of equipment and supplies on an island are always a headache, but it seems to be getting worse rather than better. And the operating costs are becoming unbelievable."

The Dive King shakes his head and goes back to check the air compressors. He has a big group going out tomorrow. And his top assistant quit yesterday. And a shipment of necessary gear and spare parts is three weeks overdue. Ah, paradise.

If only we could turn back calendars.

The turtle, almost extinct by 1900, is once again becoming very important to the economy of the Cayman Islands. Mariculture, Ltd., the world's only green sea turtle farm, was established on Grand Cayman in 1968. Centuries ago large numbers of green turtles nested on the island's broad beaches and grazed on the turtle grass found in its numerous shallow bays and sounds. In a journal dated in 1643, Captain William Jackson wrote, "These islands are much frequented by English, Dutch, and French ships that come purposely to salt up the flesh of these tortoises. The meat of the big 300 pound green turtles is sweet and tender, some part of it eating like chicken, some like veal."

During the months of May, June, and July the turtles came ashore to lay their eggs, eighty to ninety at a time, three times in a season, always in the sandy beaches. Jackson wrote further, "The females come ashore in the night only, when they must be watched without making any noise or having any light. As soon as the turtles land, the men turn them on their backs, then haul them above the high-water mark and leave them till next morning, when they are sure to find them, for they cannot turn over again, nor move from the place."

Many medical men in the eighteenth century claimed that eating turtle flesh would restore youthful vigor, guarantee a long life, and were convinced that it healed all kinds of skin problems and infections. When they were plentiful, it is estimated that over five thousand green turtles a year were taken from the Caymans. By the end of the nineteenth century they were all gone.

But with the encouragement of Mariculture, the turtle is making quite a comeback. Sales of turtle meat, shell, oil, and leather now total over two million dollars annually. Many are sold live to the turtle factories in Key West and Marathon, where they are butchered and shipped fresh or canned. Scraps of the turtle steak are ground into a delicious "hamburger."

Although Mariculture is a commercial venture, one of its objectives is the conservation of the remaining wild green turtles. At present its supply of eggs comes from the natural rookeries of Costa Rica, Surinam, and Ascension Island. Each year a percentage of the eggs collected are returned to these breeding places as healthy year-old turtles. An aim of this program is to develop methods for supporting wild turtle populations by keeping hatchling green turtles in protective custody for the first dangerous weeks of their lives, when more than 99 percent of wild hatchlings are lost, and releasing them when they are large enough to take care of themselves.

Recently Mariculture's special projects team spent a month gathering twenty thousands eggs on Ascension Island, a rocky dot in the south Atlantic. This visit included the biggest turtle-tagging operation ever undertaken. The team tagged over four hundred turtles, noting their size, description, and peculiarities—a valuable aid to the scientists' study of turtle habits, development, and navigation. In addition, the team supervised the hatching of 5,300 eggs and "escorted" the young hatchlings into the sea beyond the ring of predatory fish waiting for them.

But Mariculture does not intend to remain dependent on natural turtle rookeries for its stock. A large pond, an artificial beach, and more than one hundred adult turtles are involved in the experimental breeding program. These captive breeders have nested repeatedly on their artificial beach, and the eggs have hatched just as well as those laid in the wild. The company expects that it will soon be independent of natural egg sources.

A green turtle begins life as a round, leathery egg about the size of a ping-pong ball. At hatching, it weighs less than one ounce and is buried two to four feet beneath the sands of the rookery beach, with hundreds of brothers and sisters. The baby turtles get out of the sand by cooperative effort; a single hatchling cannot dig its way to the surface alone. They make their way to the sea at once and swim straight offshore. The males stay at sea for life; the females return to shore only to lay their eggs.

The individual hatchling's chances of growing up to be a five-hundred-pound adult are less than one in a thousand, which is the reason its mother must lay so many eggs in the first place. The mother turtle, if she escapes being caught and turned into turtle soup, breeds once every two to three years. Nesting three to ten times in a breeding season, she may produce up to a thousand eggs.

As adults, wild green turtles eat turtle grass. In captivity, Mariculture turtles are fed grass gathered in Cayman waters by a special harvesting machine, a dry soybean pellet feed, and whole frozen fish. On this diet, they reach the ideal one-hundred-pound market weight in about three years. Over 100,000 turtles are kept in round concrete tanks on a ten-acre site with large diesel pumps providing a continuous supply of clean sea water at a rate of three million gallons per hour.

Oil from the turtles raised at Mariculture will soon be smoothing out the wrinkles and soothing the sunburn on human skins around the world. A lucrative market is developing for the light golden oil in making soap, creams, and lotions, and experiments are underway on a number of other products and uses. An important quality of the oil is that it is completely absorbed, leaving no residue on the skin.

When Columbus discovered the Cayman Islands in 1503 on his fourth and last voyage to the New World, he noted, "These small and low islands are full of tortoises, as was all the sea about, and they look like little rocks." The return of the turtles to Grand Cayman would seem to be a good omen.

The sea and the sand and the coral reefs remain as simple wonders to be enjoyed. Proud of their traditions as descendants of rugged, courageous people who for centuries have survived many hazards of nature, Caymanians look to the future with concern and confidence.

But man rather than nature seems to be the source of the present dangers.

A retired mariner, Captain Sedley Ritch is now in the retail grocery business. He's not worried about foreign people and capital coming to the Cayman Islands. "We have had good people come in and have welcomed them, and we should be quite happy to see more; we need them," he says.

Edlin Hurlstone, a building contractor, is also optimistic about the future. "Islands like ours, isolated and peaceful, are hard to come by. A lot of foreign people are looking for them to 'get away from it all.' We have a nice, quiet place here and those that come seem to like it very well."

Eric Anderson, real estate broker and owner of a car rental business, has his own personal opinion: "What type of people are we catering to? Investors, quick-vacation type of people. Most will not be interested in

Cayman for itself. Their prime interests will be money, sunshine, booze, and a good time. This is not necessarily anyone's fault but is a fact of contemporary life and must be accepted. It will be a business and holiday island; we should be thankful that we have such a product to sell."

The Cayman Islands' most significant export for the past century has been able-bodied seamen. Plantations and agriculture never got a foothold there. Instead, the islanders lived from the sea, becoming sailors, fishermen, and boat builders. Today, well over two thousand Caymanians are sailing the seas under foreign flags, many of them in responsible positions aboard small freighters, supertankers, and bulk carriers.

Keith Evans, age forty-three, is one of these seamen, an engineer on a bulk carrier vessel. He spends about one month a year at home on Grand Cayman and takes a different view of the present boom in banks, building, and hotels. "Caymanians are basically a proud, honest, easygoing yet industrious people. But we are also very naive, and this character trait has a lot to do with all this recent activity. Outsiders are telling us what is good for our people, and they are liars, selfishly and surely destroying all the good things of our simple way of life. Our leaders seem to be hypnotized by the crinkle of dollars and visions of never-ending prosperity. I come back every year to my home and family and see all these changes and I just want to cry.

"But it reminds me of a story. There's this cow that starts giving a big bucket of rich wonderful milk. Suddenly it kicks over the bucket, the milk is gone, and the cow runs into the sea and drowns. In the end, there is nothing."

An example of the growing pains of the Caymans is a recent bitter controversy on the waterfront regarding the use of container-shipping trailers. Local opposition to the trailers is by no means unique; at ports all over the world the use of trailers has been opposed by dock workers. The shippers and local merchants of course point out the advantages of trailers: shipping costs are considerably reduced, more merchandise is delivered faster, and the trailers protect the goods from damage and theft. The end result should be better service and lower prices to the consumer.

John Berjal of Tropical Shipping Company says, "Ten Caymanians cannot hold up the progress of twelve thousand citizens." The dock workers, of course, take a different view of the sacrifice of their livelihood to the cause of progress.

There are no trade unions on Grand Cayman. Unfortunately, the dispute passed the vocal level and entered a physical period. Stevedores and truckers blocked the waterfront to prevent the trailers from being moved from the dock. On several occasions the tires of an entire ship-load of trailers were slashed. Negotiations and mutual concessions eventually resolved the problem. Efficient shipping is too vital to the island's expanding economy. But blood has been drawn and many Caymanians are concerned over future labor problems, especially as an increasing number of Jamaicans immigrate to join the local work force.

Vernon Scott, a quiet, well-educated man who owns a small general store in the little village of Bodden Town on the south coast, has offered these thoughts: "The human mind is such that it often fixes its sights on improving his lot. The fisherman who rows long miles every day to the reef yearns for an outboard motor. The housewife is anxious to put aside her charcoal cooking pot in favor of a butane gas stove. A father with no education wants to send his children to school. All these things we confidently call progress, and all these things require money. If Caymanians are to progress in a sensible manner, then we must find sound and enduring means of earning money, but hopefully such en-deavors can be developed and honestly compromised so as to destroy as little as possible."

Throughout the year the islanders have lived under the shadow of nature's greatest peril, the hurricane. Their worst disaster in this century was the hurricane that ravaged Cayman Brac for three days in early November, 1932. There had been a heavy storm for two days, but it seemed to have blown itself out. Alvin Rutty, an island resident for seventy-three years, recalls, "When the winds died down and the stars came out in a clear sky, we thought it was over. But early on Wednesday the wind whipped up again and in twenty minutes grew from a calm to hurricane intensity and the barometer dropped so low that it broke. The wind was estimated at two hundred miles per hour. The sea swept over the coast, carrying huge rocks on its crest, and the wind hurled boulders, some weighing tons, through the air."

In fifty-two hours of uncontrolled violence, 109 lives were lost on Cayman Brac and every building was destroyed.

One negative factor in Grand Cayman's year-round tourist development has been the extensive interior mangrove swamps that breed mosquitoes during the summer months. Journals from the early 1900s report, "The mosquitoes render life a torture to man and beast. Every house has a smoke fire from 4 P.M., and everyone sits close to it, completely enveloped in a blinding smoke which is intensely disagreeable and makes one's eyes smart."

But in recent years a very successful research and control program has been operating so that the unpleasant pests are fast disappearing. Around Georgetown, for example, the mosquito count has been reduced from an average peak density of 35,000 mosquitoes a night to less than 150.

Alice Watler has reared a family of seven and perhaps represents the thinking of the average Caymanian. She is quite worried over current events, yet optimistic about the future. "True, there is no unemployment," she says, "but it takes a magic wand to make these little paychecks stretch far enough. Food prices seem to go up daily. Our people are selling their land for what seems today like very favorable prices. But if it keeps up, we will soon all be renters with alien landlords. And I'm concerned over the many changes in the youngsters and our family life. It's a very confusing time. But we are a strong people, and I just can't believe that we will allow the greed of a few to devour us. We want to have visitors, but we do not want the visitors to have us."

These are the islands that time forgot—for a while. Quiet islands that physically and socially are quite sensitive; they are bits of land, micro-ecologies that just might not endure too many man-made mistakes.

The clock is definitely running again.

The Treasure of Isla Domingo

Once dreams are gone, they cannot be rekindled. Such fragile, nebulous things cannot be tinkered with. You must grab them while you can, for usually you do not get a second chance.

Donald Holm

FOR MANY YEARS there have been vague rumors of the existence of an island paradise in the western Caribbean that combines rare physical beauty with an almost perfect climate, a healthy, simple economy, and a friendly, fine people—yet has remained untouched by tourism or commercial interests.

An impossible dream?

Isla Domingo is located about ninety miles off the east coast of Nicaragua. It's a relatively small island of volcanic origin with a somewhat irregular shape, only five miles long by two miles wide. From the sea, the southern portion of Domingo has the appearance of a cresting green whale, its three-hundred-foot-high backbone smooth and unbroken until it ends abruptly at a cavernous limestone cliff at the southeast tip of the island.

Tucked into the south shore is Domingo Bay and the village of Elizabethtown. And what a little harbor! It's completely landlocked except for a narrow fjord-like opening that appears to be sealed off by a fringing barrier reef. But a safe water entry is made by approaching from the west, then slipping inside the reef and down the south side of the island. No finer harbor can be found in the Caribbean, as it provides complete protection from heavy winds and seas in any direction.

The offshore barrier reef continues up the eastern windward coast of the island, which has mile after mile of brilliant white beaches. And off this eastern shore, but within the protection of the fringing reef, are several small cays of sand and coconut palms.

The northern part of the island is rugged, adding a beauty to the landscape of Domingo that has been compared to some of the Marquesas Islands of South Pacific Polynesia. A 1,250-foot summit covered with a lush rain forest drops to a jumble of lesser peaks and ridges with spurs poking toward the sea to end in some places as steep rocky cliffs. Most of the fertile farming land lies either within the small valleys tucked into the folds or in the lower-lying plains across the southern half of the island.

The climate is mild and comfortable—about as healthy as you could imagine. The average daytime temperature hovers close to eighty degrees throughout the year with a moderate humidity of around 65 percent. The trade winds blow year round. Average annual rainfall is about sixty inches, with October and November usually being the wettest months. Destructive hurricanes are almost unknown, as the island is located just far enough south to be out of the tracks of these storms.

In recent history Domingo has been in the unique situation of being claimed by five countries: Nicaragua, Costa Rica, Panama, Colombia, and the United States. Although the island's physical location suggests that it should perhaps belong to Nicaragua, its cultural ties are with the British West Indies and North America. Theoretically, it came under Spanish rule by the London Treaty of 1786. And then a few years later when Spain's New World empire fell to pieces, the little island seemingly went by default to the new Republic of Colombia. But Nicaragua soon began protesting Colombia's right to the island, along with Costa Rica and Panama, all claiming jurisdiction based on various treaties and "understandings."

And then finally in 1914 the United States entered the picture when it was granted a ninety-nine year lease to Domingo by Nicaragua as part of negotiations regarding a then-projected trans-isthmian canal through

Nicaragua. The opening of the Panama Canal made Domingo a very strategic location as a coaling station for merchant vessels.

During World War II the island was used as a secret refueling hideaway for American submarines, and the U.S. Navy carefully removed the tiny dot from official charts. Even today, many maps do not indicate the existence of any such island.

Today, Domingo is a classic example of safety in numbers; it is virtually self-governing. With five countries claiming vague jurisdiction, not one would attempt to put a stranglehold on this little island that only asks to be left alone. So Domingo has its freedom; it is the only island in the Caribbean that governs itself with a unique self-sufficiency that requires no outside economic help, yet provides a standard of living approaching perfection.

Domingo was first settled in 1629 by a small group of English Puritan colonists. Located almost directly on the course of Spanish merchant ships sailing from Cartagena and Portobelo to Mexico and Havana, the temptation to prey on this rich shipping proved irresistible. It was soon apparent that privateering offered much more lucrative benefits than growing cotton and tobacco. An easy market for the plunder was the Dutch ships that frequently touched at the island. So Domingo was converted into a fortified base from which buccaneering warfare could be waged against all comers.

The Spaniards finally had had enough of these English renegades masquerading as Puritan farmers and assaulted the little island with an eighteen-vessel armada in May 1645. They effected a beachhead on the rocky, lightly defended northwest shore. After a brief skirmish, the force of eight hundred soldiers marched on to Elizabethtown and massacred the five hundred defenders, giving mercy only to the women and children.

The Spaniards occupied the island for a few years but soon lost interest. For the next two hundred years, Domingo was populated by various assortments of English, Dutch, French, and American adventurers and colonialists. The strongest groups were of course the pirates and buccaneers, and Domingo became a major smuggling base for the entire western Caribbean. As we shall see later, a most important man in this early history was a wily old English freebooter by the name of

Edward Mansveldt. The unique situation of Domingo in today's world is due mainly to Mansveldt's success as a pirate's pirate.

By the mid-nineteenth century, Domingo had passed from the age of piracy to a quiet period of stable development. The settlers were sailors, fishermen, boat builders, and farmers. And their little island had all the natural ingredients required to provide a simple livelihood. The reef developments around Domingo and three other nearby shoal areas were a fishing paradise yielding an abundance of lobster and green turtle. The lush forests covering the northern slopes gave high-quality mahogany, greenheart, and fir for homes and boats. The fertile valleys and plains, together with a twelve month growing season, provided generous crops of fruits and vegetables. Herds of cattle grazed the hillsides.

The few visitors to Domingo during the 1920s and 1930s were favorably impressed by everything they saw, but especially by the personality and energy of the people. A journal reports: "They are industrious and resourceful in all occupations, and handle the axe, hammer, and plow with great skill and pleasure. These are fine people—friendly, kind, proud, honest."

As diesel power replaced steam in powering merchant vessels, the strategic location of Domingo as a fueling base was forgotten. The five nations laying claim to the little island didn't press the issue; it offered no apparent valuable natural resources such as oil, coal, bauxite, or uranium; it was just a flyspeck lost in the vastness of the sea. Besides, a strong feeling of "nationalism" made any existence other than self-government unthinkable to the Domingans.

Coconuts had been one of their major exports since about 1860. By 1900 Domingo was harvesting fifteen million nuts annually from an estimated 1.5 million trees. Most of the coconuts went to the United States. Even today, coconut production averages about six million nuts per year. In recent years a major market for the splendid fruits, vegetables, and beef of Isla Domingo has been tourist-oriented San Andrés, fifty miles away.

And of course the entrepreneurs have tried to purvey their promises of everlasting riches if only Domingo would open itself to tourism. But the Domingans aren't tempted one bit; any way you look at it, they are far better off than tourist-ravaged San Andrés. And the reason that they can afford to be so economically independent makes a rather interesting story.

For many years a puzzling question of Caribbean history has been what happened to the relatively vast treasures that pirate Henry Morgan carried away in his infamous sacking of Panama. It is known that Morgan used Isla Providencia as an operating base in the 1670s before he turned legitimate and became the governor of Jamaica. Many believed that the majority of his Panama treasure was hidden on Providencia.

The sly old English buccaneer Edward Mansveldt was also operating in this area of the Caribbean during these years, and he used Domingo as his base. Not only were Morgan and Mansveldt competitors in the freebooting business, but they had an intense personal dislike for each other. In the summer of 1676, Mansveldt apparently pulled off the greatest coup in the history of piracy: a small fleet of his fast sailing vessels slipped into Catalina Harbor at Providencia and after a brief encounter took control of the well-fortified island. He was able to do this with relative ease because Morgan was off on a trip to Jamaica with most of his ships and men. Mansveldt held the island only a short time—but apparently long enough to locate and sail away with the bulk of the Panama riches.

But once again this treasure disappeared. For almost three centuries there was no indication of what had actually happened to this vast fortune.

Until the fall of 1946. A week of heavy rains on Domingo developed some landslides on the limestone cliffs at the southeast tip of the island. Several small passageways were opened by this act of nature, and investigation revealed two cavernous rooms. And there it was—the loot of Panama—over twenty million dollars' worth of gold, silver, and precious stones!

The conservative investment of this fortune provides an annual income to Domingo of around one million dollars—a healthy sum to support various community projects and programs, but not enough to tempt the two thousand islanders to sit back and do nothing in their own support. And the principal is untouched, making this income perpetual.

In this small community where almost everyone is a landowner, farmer, and fisherman, there is no sign of either wealth or poverty.

Homes are simple, but very comfortable, cottages and bungalows of local wood and stone with shaded yards planted with bougainvillea, hibiscus, and other tropical plants.

The people's one paramount appeal is that in domestic affairs they be left alone. "We are," one islander said to me, "more civilized than most mainlanders, both physically and socially. Literacy is 100 percent; we have excellent schools and teachers. Our people have good habits of personal cleanliness and health so that sickness is rare. On this island, you can live to a happy, ripe old age."

The occasional visitor agrees that the islanders are warm, honest, and hospitable. The children are extraordinarily well behaved. Crime is nonexistent, so a police force is completely unnecessary. No taxes of any type are levied on the people; government activities are supported completely by income from the Mansveldt treasure.

The well-integrated community life of the islanders revolves around the closely-knit family units and the church. Adult classes are available in home economics, nutrition, and handicrafts. A good export market has been developed in fine leatherwork, wood carvings, and macramé. Amateur musical and theatrical programs are very popular. The Domingans work hard, yet love a good time. They consume a moderate amount of a locally produced light rum made from their own sugar cane. Cigarette smoking is almost unknown, in spite of the fact that two centuries ago the little island was shipping substantial quantities of tobacco to Europe.

Close kinship and cultural ties still link Domingo to the English-speaking Protestant community of the western Caribbean that extends from Jamaica to the Miskito Cays off Nicaragua and includes the Bay Islands, Cayman Islands, San Andrés, and Providencia. Although Domingans have been accused of being isolationists, theirs is more a case of respect for their own privacy while maintaining a reasonable contact with the outside world. They retain ties with friends of common interests, but refuse to get involved politically in other islands' affairs that they feel are none of their business.

The Domingans are extremely cautious of visitors; very few are invited, and absolutely no "tourists" are permitted. In past years they have had unfortunate experiences with outsiders—people often with good intentions but usually trying to impose undesired values from the mainland. Domingo is a tiny, rather delicate spot, and the residents are quite aware that it would take very little to unbalance their peaceful equilibrium; they have witnessed the recent tragedies of San Andrés and Grand Cayman. It's not that visitors would be unwelcome or that the Domingans are selfish, but rather that an influx of outsiders and strangers to their community could easily destroy their treasure.

The message from these people seems to be that it is still possible for each of us to live on his own "Domingo" with genuine personal values of warmth, friendship, honesty, and simplicity, that life can actually be very fulfilling and adventurous without complexity.

The Domingans fully appreciate and are thankful for their unique position in today's confused world. And with their intense devotion to their island, they are determined to preserve the way of life that they value so highly. The quietness of Isla Domingo is broken only by the rustling of the trade winds, the faint roar of the reef, the singing of children, and the soft laughter of happiness and contentment.

They are neither going to sleep nor going to pieces.

I spent six years exploring the islands of the eastern Caribbean, searching —consciously and subconsciously—for the "perfect" island. And, of course, it was never quite there . . . at least by the standards that I considered important. So then I spent another year roaming the western Caribbean, visiting the San Blas Islands, Corn Islands, San Andrés, Providencia, Bay Islands, and the Caymans. Most had many fine positive features, but all stopped a bit short of my Utopia, with varying negative factors—political, social, economic, or physical.

So Isla Domingo is a composite of many positive elements. It could very easily exist; historically and physically all of the ingredients are most certainly out there. It just so happens that they weren't actually put together into this one particular little island. Except by me.

True paradise is perhaps a state of mind. For me, Domingo is very real.

The Boat Didn't Want to Go to Florida

AFTER SEVEN YEARS of cruising in the Caribbean, the time had unfortunately arrived to head for Florida and "regroup." The cruising kitty was just about depleted, and *Tumbleweed* needed some relatively expensive refitting and repairs.

We'd just spent a great year exploring the out-of-the-way western Caribbean and were anchored in snug little Buccaneer Cove on the south coast of Grand Cayman Island. It would be about a six-hundred-mile passage up to Key West around the western end of Cuba through the Yucatán Channel, probably a week or so depending on the weather.

A Wednesday departure was delayed, but by Friday morning I was reasonably ready to sail. The weather looked pretty good, with the normal easterly trades blowing about fifteen knots.

My good Caymanian friend Tony Nichols, a fisherman, came alongside as I was taking down the sun awning, and he climbed aboard for a cup of coffee.

"You're surely not leaving today, are you?" asked Tony. "And where's Susie, your girl friend?"

I informed him that yes, I was leaving today, and that Susie had flown off to New York earlier in the week to accept a job with an advertising agency.

Tony shook his head. "Any way you look at it, this is no time to leave Cayman—and certainly not alone. Your spirits are low; besides, the moon is completely wrong. It's new and for the next ten days will be on the make. A hungry, growing moon just about always brings mean weather this time of the year."

111

He looked around at the boat with an experienced eye. "She's not ready for a rough passage," he said. "That rigging is in bad shape; the hull is leaking like a sieve; there's a rotten place in your mainmast; and the engine doesn't run. Besides, today's Friday, and only a damn fool would start a passage on a Friday."

I acknowledged that *Tumbleweed* and I had seen better times. But that talk about moon weather and Friday departures was just old fishermen's tales and a lot of baloney. I was determined to leave today.

As we cleared Southwest Point, Tony was standing there, waving goodbye but still shaking his head.

The wind piped up that afternoon to about twenty-five knots, and some pretty fair-sized seas began building. We were running under working jib and small mizzen staysail, and the old ketch was really barreling along, although green water was breaking regularly into the cockpit. Just before dark, the main shaft sheared off on the self-steering wind-vane gear. There was no way to repair it at sea, so it meant steering the boat myself while on the run to the Yucatán Channel. After turning the corner at the west end of Cuba, we'd probably be hard on the wind up the Straits of Florida to Key West and the boat could be trimmed and balanced to steer herself.

As the wind and seas picked up, so did the bilgewater. The garboard seams had been a problem for some time; I had done some underwater caulking and patching back at Grand Cayman, and I hoped that these leaks had been slowed. But they hadn't.

I kept pretty busy that night steering and pumping.

We rounded Cape San Antonio about 11:00 P.M. the following night after a rather wild but fast day of running with only a small jib. In the lee of Cuba I raised the reefed main and mizzen, trimmed everything for going to weather on a starboard tack, and then conked out in the cockpit, pretty well exhausted. But we were almost halfway to Florida in less than two days!

I awoke about 3:00 A.M. to the luffed-out, violent flapping of all three sails. The culprit was the jib—most of the luff hanks had been torn loose. I secured the jib, then lowered the main so that I could lay hove-to with the mizzen. While securing the main, the topping lift wire broke and the heavy boom hit me a solid blow on the head across the left ear, cutting me badly. I felt warm blood running down my shoulder and crawled back into the cockpit and collapsed.

At dawn I awoke with a splitting headache and found quite a bit of dried blood caked over most of my head and upper body. A trickle of fresh blood still oozed from my ear. I realized that I hadn't eaten anything in forty-eight hours, yet I wasn't hungry. But I drank a can of juice to get something in my stomach, then went to the foredeck to see if there was any damage to the jib other than the ripped-off hanks.

And then I felt quite sick to my stomach and threw up over the bow. The emerging liquid was bloody-red; it was apparent that I must be really seriously injured—there was internal bleeding.

Weakly, I crawled back to the cockpit. It looked like maybe this was to be my last passage. I heard the sound of singing canaries and wondered if this could be the initial phase of death.

But it wasn't, because perched on the top spoke of the wheel was a bright yellow sea canary, happily singing away. He flew to the top of the binnacle, then down into the cabin for a thorough inspection of the vessel.

And I suddenly realized the source of my bloody vomit. I had drunk a can of tomato juice that hadn't been compatible with my two-day empty stomach! I wasn't going to die after all!

The canary brought a pattern of good luck. I recovered, cleaned up, made repairs, and got the boat moving again. And we had two glorious days and nights of beautiful soft and easy sailing. The wind was a steady six to eight knots out of the southeast so that we could easily lay a course to Key West on a close reach. Seas were flat and the boat sailed herself hour after hour, not fast, but so pleasant.

I fixed some good hot meals, took long naps, and my health and spirits returned to 100 percent. The little yellow bird seemed very happy aboard *Tumbleweed*, and I prepared him some rather sumptuous canary meals. He was fond of crushed Ritz crackers and potato chips, but his favorite was a mixture of crumbled Graham crackers and diced peanuts.

On the third morning he was gone. At first I thought he might be perched in an out-of-the-way cranny down below; but it was soon apparent that he must have flown away. But why?

Later, while cleaning up the cockpit, I found the answer. Under one corner of a cushion were the crumpled feathers and mashed body of the little yellow bird. During the night I had sat on my canary.

By noon the fine weather had changed to a series of mean and vicious line squalls. The winds were heavy and out of the northeast, dead on the nose from Key West. The Gulf Stream sea became very sloppy and disorganized; the boat strained and groaned.

And this was the weather pattern for the next two weeks—unpleasant to say the least. A series of rigging failures made it unwise to try to sail the boat except during the infrequent moderate spells between the violent weather systems. The bilge required almost constant pumping. Some days we'd make good only ten miles; several days we lost twenty miles.

But early one morning, twenty-three days out of Grand Cayman, the faintly flickering lights of Key West eventually appeared on a misty horizon, and old *Tumbleweed* finally limped into the outskirts of Florida.

Over a generous double noggin of rum, I arrived at the following conclusions:

1. Only a fool would consider starting a passage in the northwest Caribbean while the moon is on the make.

2. Only a complete damn fool would ever start a passage on a Friday.

3. Little yellow sea canaries definitely are in the same category as albatrosses. They bring good luck but must be protected and pampered. Their untimely death will most certainly result in bad weather, a poor passage, and very possibly misfortune.

4. Good old wooden boats can just about always take a lot more than their chicken skippers.

5. It will sure be a helluva long weather leg back to Bequia.

6. This just might be a good time to consider settling down on a nice little turkey ranch in West Texas and trying to make something of myself.

Epilogue: *Tumbleweed*

AS WE WALKED down the dock, the broker confided to me, "She's a sleeper, Fritz, and won't last long at this price. Just reduced from $22,500 and the owner is real anxious to sell. I don't want to press you, but I've got serious buyers coming down this weekend from L.A. and Frisco to look at her. If you like the boat, you'll probably have to move fast."

She looked sweet in the water . . . definitely the graceful lines of a fine designer's skilled hand and experienced eyes—but very tired. A long-forgotten, aging beauty apparently cast aside for a shiny new plastic toy. Bleeding hull fastenings; sagging, rusty standing rigging; blistered brightwork; mottled, chalking paint; a three-inch growth of barnacles at the waterline. The tattered remnants of a sun awning draped into the cockpit. But as we stepped on board I saw a beautiful old White Constellation compass mounted in a tarnished diamond-shaped brass binnacle and set on a weathered teak base. There was still some class left in the old girl.

Down below she was about the same: musty-smelling with yellowed paint, peeling varnish, drab and stained upholstery, blank spots where the clock, barometer, bookshelves, and other furnishings had recently been removed. But the basic fine wood and excellent joinerwork were still there.

"Putter around and take a good look at her," the salesman said. "Close her up when you're through, then come by my office and we'll do some serious talking." He gave me a knowing wink and a light slap on the shoulder. "Maybe we can squeeze the owner a little more on the price if I handle him just right. Like I said, he's real anxious."

The puppy-dog sales treatment: The clerk says, "This one's on sale today, my friend. Take it home with you overnight; if you don't like the

115

cute little thing, bring him back tomorrow. No problem. I've got lots of customers who'll want him."

I took the bait. For a couple of hours I opened lockers, lifted floorboards, looked up the masts, shook rigging. What circumstances would allow a man to so neglect and mistreat such a prized possession? Was there any chance at all that she could still be basically sound and solid? Was there still time for a glorious Indian summer before her life drew to a close?

> There is little man has made that approaches anything in nature, but a sailing ship does. There is not much man has made that calls to all the best in him, but a sailing ship does. There is little man has done, these modern days of rush and nerve-wrack—when beauty is sacrificed to Epstein hideousness and art to the monstrosity of daubers, when books are churned out as soulessly as their presses, and theater is given up to bawling shadows—there is little that man has made to inspire the future and carry on loveliness and sweetness of glorious and efficient beauty. The sailing ship does these things; even old, battered, sea-worn, and a little unsafe, there is inspiring loveliness and grand pursuit of difficult and dangerous duty about her, and loyal devotion, and steadfast noble carrying-on through all obstacles and difficulties.
>
> Alan Villiers

Then I lay down on one of the nice big bunks in the forward cabin to think a bit . . . and fell asleep for a short nap. And I had a vague happy/sad dream with a soft pleading voice saying, "Take me, Fritz. *Please* take me."

Fifteen thousand dollars would probably do it. But fifteen thousand— Jesus Christ. There was just no way. Unless . . . ? Possibly some very serious begging, some mighty lucky borrowing, a few imaginative lies, perhaps even a little discreet stealing. Maybe, just maybe . . .

The marine surveyor's report went something like this:

Type: Auxiliary offshore cruising ketch, wood construction.
Builder: Schaetzel Boatyard, Azusa, California.
Designer: John Alden   Year Built: 1935
Dimensions: L.O.A. = 39′ 8″; L.W.L. = 31′ 4″; Beam = 10′ 11″
Draft = 6′ 9″; Displacement = 13 tons, net.
Ballast = 8,000 lbs. lead keel.
Working Sail Area = 825 sq. ft.

EPILOGUE: TUMBLEWEED

General Description

This is a well-built high-performance cruising ketch of traditional design by John Alden. The hull is Port Orford cedar planking on white oak frames. Materials, construction, and workmanship are of excellent quality. The interior and exterior hull was inspected as thoroughly as possible, and no major structural defects were found. There is some minor localized wood deterioration, and a substantial number of important rigging, mechanical, and electrical deficiencies were noted.

Spars are Sitka spruce and appear to be in good condition. Standing rigging is galvanized iron and is in very poor condition. Running rigging is manila and nylon line, all of which needs to be replaced. Sail inventory is minimal and in poor condition.

The auxiliary engine is a 1947-vintage Graymarine four-cylinder gasoline engine rated at 37 hp. It currently is not in running order and apparently needs a major overhaul or replacement.

The interior accommodation plan is simple and comfortable. There are four large berths in two cabins, an enclosed toilet room, a very practical galley arrangement, and a good number of lockers and storage areas. Ventilation appears to be excellent with ten opening ports, two hatches, and a large skylight amidships.

The gear and equipment inventory is very minimal. It would seem that the previous owner has stripped the boat of almost everything of value.

The vessel appears to have received minimum maintenance and considerable neglect for a number of years. Exterior and interior paint, varnish, and furnishings are generally in a very run-down condition. An extensive renovation program, including rigging, mechanical, and electrical repairs and replacements, will be required to bring her back to "yacht condition."

Simply stated, this vessel appears to still be structurally sound and represents traditional first-class design, construction, and materials that are very seldom found in today's current production practices. But she needs an owner ready to provide the tender loving care that she deserves.

But now I looked about me and found I was in a different world. The ship was the same, yet utterly different. She was alive now instead of dead; clean, scrubbed and burnished; neat and orderly aloft and alow where before had been a disreputable confusion. The stately fabric of her seemed to possess a life of its own. She leaned or dipped to every gust of the breeze and every surge and undulation of the sea.

Rex Clements

Fifteen very good years and about 40,000 miles have slipped by. We've sailed those "balmy ever-blowing trades in a climate of perpetual springtime with legendary magical islands, secluded coves, sparkling sugar-sand beaches, gin-clear water, rustling palm trees, dusky maidens . . ."

Not the least of the various magics which take place is the bond created between a man and the boat in which he sails. It is not necessarily that between a man and a thing. After a time at sea a boat becomes more than a clever assemblage of insensitive matter. I think of a boat as a creature thing. For me she is infused with a persona, hovering on the edge of animation. It should not be difficult to understand how a yacht can become imbued with anima and personality. After all, it is a shelter and shield, however frail, and each yacht develops attributes and characteristics peculiar to herself in the way she meets the conditions and hazards of a passage. She can be cranky or sea-kindly, but in the end the man and boat are made partners in the presence of the antagonist, the sea . . . Chameleonlike she takes on the coloration of her owner's needs. Each man uses his boat in his own way to fill certain wants. There are as many roads to Nirvana as boats and men.

William Snaith

And we've also experienced those wild reinforced winter trades with their curling, cresting, breaking mixmaster seas; mean and vicious gear-busting line squalls; rolling, gut-thumping anchorages.

A lot of happy times, and a few bad ones. She's most certainly not a perfect boat, but what a fine lucky compromise!

What sentimental foolishness! I condemned to hell the unknown romanticist who originated the ridiculous fancy that a man might fall in love with a thing. And what else was a vessel but a thing? This absurd relationship between a man and his vessel would be better called a fetish than love, yet what in the end was the difference? . . .

You old bitch! I whispered.
Your butt is covered with barnacles
And your bosom sags with weeds.
Your limbs are scarred with wear
And your hair is dyed with rust.
You are demanding and expensive
And uncomfortable to live with . . .

Ernest K. Gann

And then came a single-handed passage back to the islands of the Caribbean from Florida. It was Friday; November 14. The first rays of dawn appeared in the eastern sky, the grays and blues and pinks and golds slowly developing into a friendly, happy sky. And what a fine night we'd had with easy seas and the winds blowing a moderate twelve knots or so out of the southeast. On the starboard tack, *Tumbleweed* is sailing a course of due east and averaging 5½ knots under working jib, main, and mizzen.

For the past two years I had been holed up in Florida doing extensive rebuilding, refitting, and repairs to the old girl. The hull was refastened, all standing and running rigging replaced, new sails, gear, and accessories installed, and all surfaces refinished with fresh paint and varnish. It had been a long and hard two years, laboring for dollars during the day, working on the boat nights and weekends. But *Tumbleweed* emerged once again vitally alive and sparkling with grace, dignity, and class.

We'd had a carefree summer cruising the Bahamas, and now I was on my way to the Virgin Islands to try again at some winter chartering, back to my old sailing and cruising friends and the matchless West Indies.

This morning we were seven days out of George Town, Great Exuma, and all had gone reasonably well. Although there had been about thirty hours of unstable weather three days ago, we couldn't ask for better weather now. About four hundred miles more to St. Thomas. *Hot dog! We'll easily make it by Thanksgiving!*

Then the entire eastern horizon turned a bloody crimson. *Red sky at morning, sailor take warning. And what about this "Devil's Triangle" that we're sailing in—a notorious area in the southwest North Atlantic of mysterious tragedies and strange disappearances . . . sea monsters . . . supernatural phenomena . . . Baloney! Go get 'em old weed boat!*

The sun peeked up and we had this part of the ocean all to ourselves, with only a few purple scudder clouds scattered to the east and a couple of cauliflower puffies overhead. The boat was trimmed and sailing herself fine, so I went below and started breakfast, brought the log and navigation up to date, then planned to have a nap. I was tired after being up all night keeping a lookout for freighter traffic. Not a single light had been sighted during the night. I picked up the early morning radio weather report from Puerto Rico and learned that an intense frontal system was affecting the central Bahamas "with strong winds and rough seas" and should be moving into my area later today—"twenty-five- to thirty-five-knot winds out of the northwest shifting to the north-northeast with the frontal passage." *Hey, strong northwest winds—we'll really knock off some fast reaching miles with stuff like that! Old* Tumbleweed *will eat 'em up! Look out, you Virgins!*

I tweaked the dials some more on the little shortwave receiver to find some lively breakfast music.

Things got lively, all right. There was a horrendous crash and violent slam that threw me to the cabin sole. I jolted up the companionway. To starboard was a solid black wall moving by to the west, grabbing and tearing and crushing and pounding at *Tumbleweed*'s hull and rigging. In a moment there was a last shuddering crunch and vibration as this dark monster made final contact, then rushed clear. We were left wallowing in a foamy, hissing wake with broken wood, dangling wire, and flailing sails. A fast glance astern indicated that a medium-sized freighter had apparently stopped about five hundred yards away, and a motionless man on the bridge deck gazed down at me.

The masts were swaying dangerously. *I've got to get those sails off . . . slack all sheets . . . lower halyards.* But the sails wouldn't come down! The bowsprit was badly damaged and the top couple of feet of the mainmast sheared off, jamming the jib and main halyards. Spreaders on both masts were broken and the sail track damaged, so the luff slides wouldn't come down. *Hey, check the bilge—are we making water?* Yes, the bilge was quite full, but about a hundred strokes on the big hand pump took it down a bit, so we weren't sinking.

What a mess! But the ship has stopped and will give us help. I looked for the freighter—it was almost a mile away and steaming off to the west, belching black smoke from its stack!

I pinched myself. *It's just a bad nightmare. Wake up. All is well.*

But it was for real. *Settle down and let's see what we've got.* All standing rigging for both masts on the starboard side was gone. The masts were still there, except for the top portion of the main, although both were quite wobbly and unsteady. The bowsprit was splintered and useless, the stern boomkin sheared off, so there were no fore-and-aft

120

stays to support either mast. Six holes were torn in the starboard topsides, including a long gash at the waterline and a large, jagged opening amidships. The cabin interior was a shambles with broken bulkheads, ripped open lockers, scattered gear. The little auxiliary engine was partially torn from its mounts and lying cockeyed with a broken propeller shaft coupling. *But the water—how much water are we making? Another hundred strokes of the bilge pump, so we're taking on a fair amount, but it looks like it can be handled.*

Slowly, a little order evolved. I finally got the jib halyard unsnarled and the jib lowered and secured. Main and mizzen were a problem with the damaged track; it would require going aloft to get them down. I slid the foot of each sail forward off its boom and secured the lower portions by brailing around the masts. Much better, but there was still a lot of free sail beating aloft. I rigged some crude shroud and stay supports for both masts with wire, line, and clamps. Certainly an improvement, even though the spars were continuing to bend quite a bit. *If the weather stays good, I can do a better job later.*

I checked the bilge often; water seemed to be entering the boat at about 150 gallons per hour. I went over the side with a face mask and examined the underwater hull; there appeared to be a lot of seam damage, especially along the garboard planking. The old hull had really been twisted and wracked by the collision. There were two serious openings— the hole at the waterline and a badly damaged spot on the lower bow. I crudely filled both areas with rags, caulking cotton, and a two-part epoxy patching compound. The water flow into the boat seemed to be cut almost in half.

Let's see what we can do with that wild mainsail up there. I rigged my gantline going-aloft tackle to the only halyard left—the old spinnaker pole topping lift, three-eighths-inch nylon line that didn't look too good. It was a struggle to pull myself up the wobbly spar, with the boat rolling quite a bit more than I had figured. I continually smashed into the mast and rigging as I inched myself upward to the lower spreaders about twenty-five feet off the deck where I could unshackle slides above the damaged track and get that main down. Almost there . . . then *whoooosh* and *plawwwwwp* . . . and I hit the deck like a ripe tomato. The old halyard had failed. I was momentarily stunned, then in intense

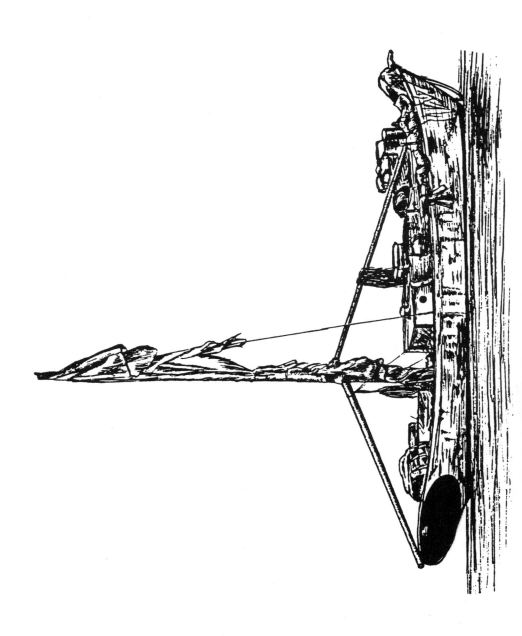

pain. *Every bone in my body must be broken.* But slowly feeling returned and I found that all limbs seemed to be intact and would move. I had hit on top of the forward hatch, the only clear spot on the foredeck, surrounded by the protruding, pointy edges of three anchors, samson posts, and debris. My luck wasn't completely bad.

I crawled back to the cockpit and contemplated the situation seriously. Things weren't good, but they could surely have been worse. The old girl was still afloat. And given enough time with good weather, I should be able to put together some kind of a jury rig to sail downwind. There could be no powering, as the auxiliary engine was useless. The closest harbor with decent protection was the little island of South Caicos, about 160 miles to the west-southwest. *But the weather report says that this nice easy weather will soon be coming to an end.* It was now a little past noon; the wind had lightened to less than eight knots and had swung to the south, with a perceptible long swell coming in from the northwest. *Some rough weather might finish us off. I think maybe we could use some help.* Discretion sometimes is the better part of valor. *Let's see if the old radiotelephone can make a contact.*

The regular antenna had been carried away, so I hung a jury-rig wire between the two masts as far up as I could reach. A poor arrangement, but maybe it would get out some kind of a signal. "This is an emergency call from the forty-foot ketch *Tumbleweed.* I am in a disabled condition after being struck by a hit-and-run freighter. Hull and rigging are badly damaged; the auxiliary engine is not operational. I require assistance. My location is approximately 23°-10′ North, 68°-55′ West. Repeat . . ." I sent this message over my three working frequencies of 2182, 2638, and 2738 kc on the little 45-watt transmitter.

There was no response from any of them. The battery was in fair shape, but I decided I'd better not waste it. I would try again later.

I attempted to beef up the rigging but could only rig lower shrouds on the masts without going aloft. *If I could only climb those sticks, get the sails down, and hang on some decent support.* But there was just no way. A very painful soreness was developing in my lower back, buttocks, and legs.

By mid-afternoon a light new breeze was coming from the west and a large swell was building up out of the northwest. I tried the radio again. There was a very weak response from the motor vessel *Robert Conrad*: "*Tumbleweed*, we received your earlier transmission and have relayed it to the Coast Guard at San Juan. Are you in immediate danger?"

"No," I answered back, "but I am disabled. I'm taking on water, but so far have it under control. Rough weather could make my condition quite serious."

A faint garble, static, then nothing more.

By twilight the wind was blowing fresh from the northwest with a sky full of angry black clouds, and large seas were building. We lay beam-to, the two sails flogging fiercely; if only they'd come to pieces. But they were strong, well-made dacron sails and seemed amazingly indestructible. We rolled and wallowed and pitched, with the masts working a lot. My body ached; I tried to eat something, but nothing would stay in my stomach.

By 9:00 P.M. it was blowing very hard and raining, and heavy seas were throwing the hull around quite violently. Then I heard the snap and twang of breaking wire—the remaining standing rigging on both spars was gone. For the next three hours the main and mizzen masts wracked and swayed and bent and twisted in an unbelievable display of strength and contorted rhythm. I crouched in the companionway peeking through the hatch. The wind was howling and shrieking, lightning flashing, green water and heavy spray cascading over the helpless boat. I could do nothing except wait for the inevitable and hope that when the spars finally came crashing down, they wouldn't cause total destruction.

Just before midnight the wild dance ended and both masts collapsed within a few minutes of each other. The main broke into two pieces, leaving a three-foot stub still intact on the foredeck; the section to the first spreaders lay over the crushed starboard rail, half in the water, half on the splintered deck. The top section was in the water on the lee side, pounding into the hull, still spider-webbed to the boat by a tangle of wire, line, and sail. The mizzen mast, broken in two at the spreaders and hinged by track, sail and halyard, was swinging wildly through the air. The shattered bowsprit with pulpit broke loose and was beating into the bow below the waterline, still attached by the bobstay chain and one whisker stay.

It was one helluva mess, and the weather continued to be nasty.

Through the rest of the night I crawled around, trying to secure pieces of debris, crudely plugging up the gaping deck holes with rags and canvas, and placing fenders, cushions, and lifejackets along the lee hull where the hunk of spar in the water was pounding into the sides and trying mercilessly to destroy its old partner.

And I pumped a lot of water. Leakage was increasing considerably as the weather deteriorated. Over half my time was spent pumping. What a night!

At dawn I was finally able to see what I was doing and started cutting wire and lines and track and sail to get that bloody mast loose from the boat. But first of all I rigged another antenna wire and tried a final series of radio transmissions, indicating my current situation. Nothing came back except faint, whistling static. The battery was just about dead.

Unknown to me at the time, however, I did get out another weak signal that was relayed to Coast Guard San Juan. At 9:00 A.M. that Saturday morning, a 182-foot cutter left Puerto Rico heading for my estimated position, 350 miles away. It was a needle-in-a-haystack search mission.

The mast section was finally cut loose. But that crazy maverick circled the stern and came up along the weather port side and started whacking away at virgin wood! I finally found and cut the one wire that still held it to the boat. The defiant hunk of spruce appeared to sail away straight upwind with a jagged spreader waving triumphantly in the air; it seemed to say, "So long, you reaching fool. I tried for years to make you go to weather, but you just would never learn!"

For the next thirty hours the weather gods continued their onslaught. By late Sunday afternoon I was running out of steam; my back throbbed with increasing pain. Almost constant pumping was required, and I was beginning to lose ground as water sloshed well above the floorboards. Things didn't look so good. I loaded the little eight-foot dinghy that was lashed on the cabin top with a survival kit of food, water, flares, and its small sailing rig. The 160 miles downwind to the nearest island would be a sporty passage in this weather, but with a bit of luck I should be able to make it.

125

I tried to pump harder and harder, but the bilge water slowly gained. When the water began lapping at my knees, it was apparent that the struggle was hopeless; there was just no way that I could keep her afloat through another night. Soon I would have to give up and take to the dinghy.

I was going to lose my faithful old friend.

Then, just before dark, a small ship came out of a mean squall line to the southeast. I waved and shouted and laughed and cried and prayed. It was the Coast Guard cutter *Sagebrush* plunging and pitching and rolling across a wild prairie of water toward a rescue rendezvous with a desperate *Tumbleweed*—mangled, torn, splintered, bleeding—but she was still alive.

You old bitch, I tearfully whispered . . .